SLIPPERY JACK

SLIPPERY JACK

10,000 Authentic Names, Nicknames, and Aliases From the Old West 1870-1910

DENNIS MCCOWN
("SEVEN LADDERS")

Copyright © 2016 Dennis McCown
All rights reserved.

ISBN: 0692726292
ISBN 13: 9780692726297
Library of Congress Control Number: 2016909376
Bent Sun Productions, Lockhart, TX

OTHER BOOKS BY DENNIS MCCOWN

A biography:

> **The Goddess of War**: A True Story of Passion, Betrayal, and Murder in the Old West

A novel (as novelist Butch Denny):

> **Savage Winter**: A Story of Wilderness ... and Survival

TABLE OF CONTENTS

Other Books by Dennis McCown	v
Foreword	ix
Thoughts on These Names	xiii
How to Use This Compilation	xv
Biblical names	1
Perfectly good Biblical names <u>not</u> encountered in Old West Research:	7
Men's Names	9
Famous figures from history, geography, mythology, or things:	9
Literature, Myth and Legend:	12
Rank or Title:	13
Characteristics:	13
Religious names, not necessarily from the Bible:	16
Names derived from surnames:	17
Names derived from the English language or culture:	22
Black Men's Names	31
Hispanic Men's Names	32
California/Arizona	32
New Mexico	34
Texas	35

Men's Nicknames	37
Names derived from places:	37
Names derived from characteristics:	39
Famous Men's Nicknames	43
Miscellaneous:	50
Women's Given Names	61
Names derived from Characteristics:	62
Names derived from History, Literature, or the Bible:	63
Names derived from stones/precious stones:	63
Names derived from places:	64
Names derived from flowers:	66
Common Women's Names	67
Other common Women's Names:	101
Women's Nicknames	126
Famous Women's Nicknames of the Old West	128
Names and Nicknames of Women of "Easy Virtue"	130
Famous Names or Nicknames:	130
Names of the Not-So-Famous:	131
Black Women's Given Names	134
Hispanic Women's Given Names	135
Miscellaneous Women's Names:	137
Surnames	138
Descriptive Names	141
Alternative Names for Whiskey—	141
Alternative Names for Bars—	142
Unusual Names	148

FOREWORD

During research for my book *The Goddess of War, A True Story of Passion, Betrayal, and Murder in the Old West,* I discovered a number of interesting names, nicknames, and aliases of the Old West. I also joined the Single Action Shooting Society, whose members adopt monikers in a Western tradition. Many SASS members have told me it was difficult to come up with a good alias, as "all the good ones are taken." Sure enough, "Wild Bill" Hickok and "Calamity Jane" were chosen long ago. With that in mind, I decided to research and list typical names of the period 1870-1910 as a guide for screenwriters, novelists, reenactors, budding parents, SASS members, and others.

To my surprise, names I thought were common … were not. Wyatt, for example, is rare in the Old West, but Wellborn or Welborn is common. Larkin is more common than Lawrence. At the time, initials were commonly used too, especially the first two like W.C. Williams, rather than William Crawford Williams.

So, I had to decide what kind of names to include in this book. The Old West was rich with particular *groups* of names:

1.) Native American (or Indian) names. A fertile field here, but the names deserve lots of explanations. There are also many spelling variants, so, for the most part, I'll leave Native American names to someone else to research.
2.) Alien names. I decided to merely touch on these, for there were so many cultures represented in the West including German, Chinese, Polish, Wendish, Welsh, Italian, Norwegian, and others.
3.) African-American (black): Pre- or post-Civil War? Plus the fact that blacks were poorly documented and educated, leading to many spelling problems, so I decided to scratch the surface on this subject and leave it for others to mine.
4.) Spanish/Hispanic (Mexican): What a rich field this is, but again, I decided it is, for the most part, outside my expertise in this slim volume.

At the same time, another crossroads confronted me about halfway through this compilation: How was I to *organize* this guide, and what was my purpose in doing so? My basic premise—that I wanted the guide to be interesting as well as fun—would best be served by its organization. I drew up a couple lists of two thousand names each, one alphabetized, the other in random order. I circulated the lists among friends, warning I would check back in a week. Actually, I allowed them two weeks, then gave a "pop quiz." Not a single person given an alphabatized list read more than a page or two. Their overwhelming opinion: "boring." Readers with random lists, however, read all the names, and I questioned them closely about what they recalled. Apparently, a random list stimulated an appreciation of each name's uniqueness. These readers reported an occasional chuckle or even a guffaw. Most remembered a few of the names, whereas the "alphabetical people" couldn't recall even one. Therefore, my compilation's purpose—to be interesting as well as fun—would best be suited in random order. That is not to say there is no order. I tended to group related names together, hence Opal, Jewel, Pearl, and Ruby are in a mini-grouping.

As you read the nicknames section, it might prove enjoyable to "play" with a name like Tom, Dick, or Harry. Nicknames like One-Eye, Salt Lick, or Black are just nicknames when you read them, but add a name like Tom and you get One-Eyed Tom, Salt Lick Tom, or Black Tom—and more fun. That's what my compilation is all about: fun. I hope you enjoy the wonderful variety and sheer fun of these names of the Old West.

Finally, I did not even try to catalog the names of horses or Judas longhorns. This is a hugely imaginative field—but the documentation is either sparse, unreliable, or unprovable. Sometimes, it's even … unprintable! My favorite, you must understand, however, is a horse named "Old Paint." I'm from Cheyene; I have always missed it, but in Alta Vista Elementary School, as obedient children, we were taught to sing:

I ride an Old Paint
And leading Old Dan.
I'm going to Montana,
For to throw the hoolihan.

They feed in the coulee
And they water in the draws.
Their tails are all matted,
And their backs are all raw.

Goodbye Old Paint.
I'm a leaving Cheyenne.
Goodbye Old Paint.
I'm a leaving Cheyenne.

I did leave Cheyenne, but it'll always be in my heart—as will the Old West. I hope you enjoy these wonderful, authentic names from the Old West!

—Dennis McCown
Registered in SASS, the Single Action Shooting Society, as "Seven Ladders," #75152, a name honoring legendary cowboy Martin Mrose's cattle brand in Seven Rivers, New Mexico, a brand the author "keeps up" as his own today.

THOUGHTS ON THESE NAMES

Nicknames in our world don't have the fun about them that names in the Old West had. There's something playful and appealing about cowboys named "Stump," "Baldy," or "Bug." There's no such fun today.

Many given names common today were also comon then. John, David, Robert, Mary, Laura, and Susan, for example, were common. Such names are, for the most part, not included in this collection. At the same time, ethnic names are also excluded. During this period, the United States was a land of immigrants. Foreign first names like Gottfried, Wilhelmina, and Werner appeared all over the West—leading of course to the wide-spread use of nicknames and aliases. For example, your *compadre* sitting beside you at a amoky campfire at a sheep-camp in wintry southern Utah would not be known as Werner Otto Schnitzeldorff, his given name, but as "Dutch Charlie."Or the man you bought a couple turkeys from wasn't Theodosius Sessumshickerd, but "Turkey Tom." It made things easier and perhaps helped with assimilation. We don't observe this phenomenon today with the large numbers of Hispanic immigrants, but we do see it with Chinese newcomers. It is for that reason a young woman toiling away at a computer in the cubicle next to you in a corporate headquarters in Chicago calls herself "Sue," rather than her real name of Hswieh.

To compensate for bad spelling and illiteracy, I have only listed spellings I've seen at least <u>five</u> times, unless otherwise noted.

A note on discrimination for future researchers. Though the job market now is increasingly homogenized with Internet application forms and reliance on Social Security numbers as "levelers," recent African-American sub-cultural naming will affect job-hiring discrimination. Thus a woman named LaQuirsha or Tamickacharmaine or a man named Sirgeourge Prince can be discriminatorily excluded from job consideration simply because of their names, not by the interview process. Research will need to be conducted into this phenomenon using the 2000 and 2010 censuses, when released.

HOW TO USE THIS COMPILATION

Dashes, slashes, brackets, and parentheses are used extensively through the lists, and it's important the reader know what they mean.

Dashes denote nicknames. Hence:

> Nathan—Nate
> Abigail—Abbie
> Edward—Ed or Eddie

Slashes are alternate spellings. The spelling encountered most often is listed first. Lesser spellings are listed afterward. Hence:

> Enoch/Enouch/Enock
> Ferrel/Farrell/Farrall
> Brazos/Brazis

Brackets are used for notes or comments. Hence:

> Bull [not encountered as a nickname for people, but turned up as a nickname for a horse!]

Sarah/Sara—Sadie—[Often used with a middle name. e.g. Sarah Jane]

Parentheses are used for names the author encountered only once during research, but they were so descriptive, they were included. Hence:

Cecilia—Sissy/Sissie (or Cissy)

Dashes, slashes, brackets, and parentheses can be used in the same entry. Hence:

Augustus/Agustis/Agustus—Gus/Guss (or Gust or Gusty/Gustie) [A memorable character in Larry McMurtry's western novel Lonesome Dove.]

BIBLICAL NAMES

There was a period in England, later exemplified by the Puritans and others in America, when Biblical names were common. To a small extent, three factors influenced the use of Biblical names in the Old West: culture, connotation, and frequency.

First culture. Foreign-sounding names from the Bible—despite their positive connotations—were, for the most part, unacceptable. Therefore such worthy names as Amashai, Anab, Engedi, Huzoth, Jerrubbesheth, Nophah, Shishak, and Zerubbabel never made it into common usage.

Second, connotation. Perfectly good names like Goliath, Satan, Saul, and Judas are, in my research, unseen. And Jezebel? Oops, not in the Old West! Other names are not seen until the modern era like Sharon and Ophrah. And other great names like Jeezer and Azriel? Not in the Old West. Shiloh, Memphis, Nebo, and Ophir remain places, not personal names; Roman and Omar are Hispanic; Nimrod became a common noun—but not a name— for a hunter. Demetrius and Quartus are overwhelmingly Latin/Roman.

Third, frequency. Due to the cyclical nature of sermons and messages in the Christian year, some names are repeated in annual messages to congregations, therefore names like Paul, David, and others appear with more frequency and were more likely to be accepted.

Author's Favorite: Uriah

Men's and women's biblical names in alphabetical order that are encountered in the Old West:

Aaron
Abel
Abigail—Abbie/Abby
Abijah
Abilene
Abner—Ab
Abraham—Abram or Abe or Ab
Absolam or Absalum (Absilium)—Ab
Adah/Ada
Adam
Aeneas
Ahab
Alexander—Alex or Alec/Aleck
Amos
Anna
Andrew—Andy or Drew
Asa
Ashbel
Augustus/Agustis/Agustus—Gus (or Gust or Gusty/Gustie) [A memorable character in Larry McMurtry's novel Lonesome Dove.]
Ava
Balaam
Barnabas
Bartholomew—Bart
Benjamin—Ben
Bethany—Beth
Beulah/Beula/Bulah/Bula
Cain [!]

Caleb—Cale
Candace [Candy seems to be 1910+]
Chloe
Claudia
Clement—Clem
Cornelius
Cyrus (The Persian for this, Kouroush, never appears.)
Damaris
Daniel—Dan or Danny
Darius (The Persian for this, Dariush, never appears)
Deborah/Debora {Debby is 1910+]
Delilah/Delila
Demetrius
Dorcas
Drucilla/Drusilla—Dru
Elam
Eleazer/Eliezer
Eli
Elias
Elihu/Eligu
Elijah
Elisha
Elizabeth
Emmanuel
Enoch/Enouch
Enos
Erastus—Rastus
Esther
Ethan [but not Etham, which appears to be non-Biblical]
Eve
Ezekiel—Zeke
Felix
Festus

Gabriel—Gabe
Gideon
Hannah
Herod/Herrod
Hezekiah
Hiram—Hi
Immanuel [Emmanuel variation]
Ira
Isaac
Isaiah (Osiah)
Jacob [not encountered often in the Old West--though popular today]
James—Jim or Jimmy
Jedediah—Jed
Jemimah/Jemima
Jeremiah
Jeroboam
Jerusha
Jesus [mostly Hispanic. Pronounced Hey-sus in Spanish.]
Jesse/Jessie [Often a nickname for Jesus]
Jethro
Joab
Joel
John
Jonathan [often abbreviated Jno.]
Joseph—Joe or Jo
Joshua
Josiah—Joe or Jo
Jubal
Judah
Judith
Julius
Keturah/Ketura/K'turah [K'turah was my grand-aunt's name, about 1900.]
Kezia
Leah

Lemuel—Lem
Levi
Lois
Lucas [but not Luke]
Macedonia [Mace seems to be the shortened form]
Magdalena [Overwhelmingly Hispanic. A variant, Magdalene, is uncommon]
Mahala/Mahalah [Common, especially among blacks.]
Malachi
Marcus/Mark
Mariam/Miriam
Martha
Martin
Mary [Maria with many spelling variants]
Matthew—Matt
Melita
Micah
Mordecai
Moriah
Moses
Myra
Nathan—Nate/Nat
Nathaniel/Nathanael/Nathaneel—Nate
Nicholas/Nicolas
Noah
Nora/Norah
Obadiah/Obediah/Obedia (O.B.)
Obed
Omar
Paul
Peter—Pete or Pety/Petey
Phebe
Philemon (Pronounced File-E-mon)
Phillip/Philip—Phil
Phineas

Priscilla
Rachel
Reba
Rebecca—Becky or Becka/Becca
Reuben
Rezin
Rhoda
Roman [overwhelmingly Hispanic]
Ruth
Rufus—Rufe
Salem
Salma
Samuel—Sam
Sarah/Zerah [Many variants]
Selah/Sela
Seth
Smamrach/Shemrach—Sham
Silas—Si
Simeon/Simon/Simeon—Si
Solomon/Solaman—Sol
Stephen—Steve
Sud/Sudie
Susannah/Susanna
Tabitha
Thomas—Tom or Tommy [Tomas in Hispanic cultures]
Titus
Thaddeus—Thadd or Thad
Uriah
Veronica
Zachariah/Zechariah/Sechariah—Zach/Zake
Zabediah/Zabadiah/Zebadiah/Zebediah/Sebediah—Zeb or Seb
Zebulon/Zebulon—Zeb

PERFECTLY GOOD BIBLICAL NAMES <u>NOT</u> ENCOUNTERED IN OLD WEST RESEARCH:

Azriel
Chloe
Diana/Dinah
Eunice/Eunis/Unis
Eve
Ezekiel   [very 1920s, but not Old West]
Goliath
Ham
Herod
Ichabod
Ishmael   [Moby Dick didn't become popular until 1890s+]
Jericho
Jason   [So popular today it's become trite]
Job
Judas
Jupiter
Lazarus
Memphis
Mercurius
Meshach
Mammon
Mordeci
Nebo
Nimrod
Ophir
Reba
Salma
Salome
Samson

Satan [except for broncs and bulls]
Saul
Shiloh
Seraphim
Sharon
Sheba
Silvanus

MEN'S NAMES

Author's Favorite: Booker

Note: In looking through historical records, remember that a good percentage of the people were illiterate. Hearing the names, census takers, county clerks, and newspaper editors may not have copied, used, or transcribed spellings correctly. Therefore, alternate spellings listed here may not be accurate, but since the author ran across them several times, they are noted anyway.

FAMOUS FIGURES FROM HISTORY, GEOGRAPHY, MYTHOLOGY, OR THINGS:

Americus
George Washington
Washington—Wash
Thomas Jefferson
Jefferson—Jeff

Zachariah Taylor
Andrew Jackson
Jackson—Jack
Lincoln—Link
Grant
Jeff Davis—Jeff
Benjamin Franklin
DeWitt Clinton
Oliver Perry
Daniel Webster
Layfayette/Lafayette/Lafaett/Layfayett—Fayette
Plato
Marcellus
Leonidas
Silvanus
Theophulas/Theophilas
Beauregard/Boregard/Boreguard/Borgard (Bauregard)
Raleigh/Rauligh
Rashleigh
Jerry Dunn
Columbus
Osceola
Powhattan
Caddo
Dallas
Seguin   [A name popular after the Texas Revolution]
Austin   [A name popular after the Texas Revolution]
Travis   [A name popular after the Texas Revolution]
Travis   [A name popular after the Texas Revolution]
Crockett/Crocet   [A name popular after the Texas Revolution]
Waco

Napolean/Napolian/Napulien
Bonaparte—Bony
Wellington
Darius
Cicero
Julius
Caesar
Flavius/ Flavious
Pompey
Scipio/Cipio/Sipeo
Titus
Horace/Horice/Horus/Horrace
Marcellus
Sosthenes
Augustus/Agustis/Agustus—Gus/Guss or Aug (or Gust or Gusty/Gustie)
    [It's possible the nickname "Windy" comes from Gusty.]
Octavius/Octavus
Sixtus—Sixey
Socrates
Solon
Nero
Lycurgus/Licurgus
Virgil/Virgel/Virgle—Gil or Virg
Leander
Cicero
Ovid
Homer
Cato
Cyrus/Syrus/Cyras
Veto
Leonidas—Leon

Hannibal
Medicus
Hamlet
Monday
January
July
Adelius
Cornelius/Cornelious
Lucien/Lucian
Coffee/Cuffey
Valentine/Valantine
Leondidas/Leonides
Secunday/Secuanday
Isaac Newton
Prosper/Prospero
Marcellus
Balthazar/Baltazar
Lucius

LITERATURE, MYTH AND LEGEND:

Achilles
Mars/Mar
Ulysses/Ulyses/Ulysus/Ullisis
Cupid
Septimus
Hector
Bede
Aesop/Asap
Romeo
Janus

Croesus/Croeasus
Orion/Oreon
Lysander
Claudius /Claudious

RANK OR TITLE:

Commodore/Comodore
Prince
King
Colonel
Major
General
Squire
Teacher   [A name, not merely a title]
Doctor—Doc/Dock   [A name, not merely a title]
Governor
Queen   [Not a name you'd saddle a boy with today!]
Earl/Erl
Artillery

CHARACTERISTICS:

Nice
Sweet
Honey
Sour
Pucker
Bitter
Salty/Salt

Luscious	[Probably a variant of Lucius, pronounced LOO-shus, but common in this period and occasionally today as LUSH-us]
Pleasant	
Dumb	
Stupid	
Fat	
Tall	
Big	
Skinny	
Young	
Old/Old Man	
Elder	[Common in Mormon areas, but encountered elsewhere, too]
Younger	
Young	
Kid	
Lone	
Wily/Wiley	
Dancer	
Easy	
Rich	
Blue	
Button	
Chunk	
Lean	
Cagey—Cage	
Vice	
Hasty	[A name and a nickname]
Cry	
Justice	
Hurry	
Welcome	
Study	

Luck/Lucky—Luckey
Wiseman
Friend
Reason/Reson
Orange
Craven   [A name, not a nickname]
Smart   [A name *and* a nickname]
Early
Sterling
Welborn/Wilborne/Wellborn/Wilburn   [One of my favorite Old West books was written by Welborn Hope. What a great name!]
Finis/Fines—Finny
Trusty   [A name and a nickname]
Crest
Seaman/Seman
Vitae
Vital
Orange
Monk
Ace
Nimrod   [A Biblical name, but listed in this section since hunting was a desired characteristic on the frontier.]
Shatt   [Past and past participle of another word?!]
Shade
Phantom
Booker—Book
Warren
Creed
Seaborn/Seborn/Seaborne/Seborne—Sebe
Green
Roan
Venerable

RELIGIOUS NAMES, NOT NECESSARILY FROM THE BIBLE:

Easter
Luther—Luke
Martin Luther
John Wesley
Hesikiah
Esau
Abel/Able
Isham/Ischam
Shadrach—Shad
Reuben/Rheuben/Ruben/Rubin
Eli/Ely
Matthew/Mathew—Matt/Mat
Noah
Jonas
Elihu
Hiram—Hi or Hy
Joel
St. Elmo
St. John
St. Joe
St. Peter
St. Mark
Joseph—Joe or Jodie/Jody
Nathaniel/Nathanial—Nate or Nathan
Absolam/Absalam—Ab
Ocinath   [Have seen this as minister's names, but unsure if there is a religious connection.]
Aaron/Aron/Arin
Jerome

Noel
Micajah/Micaja
Obediah—Obed
Baptiste
Melchior/Melchor
Timothy—Tim
Azariah
Silas/Silaus/Sylas/Silous
Rufus—Rufe
Daniel—Dan or Danny
Ebenezer
Samuel/Semuel—Sam   [But not "Sammy" in this time period]
Emmanuel/Emanuel/Immanuel/Imanuel—Mannie/Manny
Asa
Sidon
Uriah
Mathias/Matias—Matt/Mat
Moriah
Tilmon/Tilman
Isam/Isom
Enos
Seton
Zebulon—Zeb
Amon/Ammon

NAMES DERIVED FROM SURNAMES:

Rupert
Essex
Hubbard

Bledsoe
Bowler
Thacker
Bedford
McDuff
Warren
Brooke
Tolbert
Dryden
Evans/ Evins
Ratliff
Turner
Shedwick
Mellville/Melville
Wilks
Dow
Bascomb
Ewing
Whorton
Leighton
Sheppard
Ewald
Stayton
Sumner
Winthrop/Winthrup/Winthrope
Porter
Sedgwick
Pickens
Tapley
Wheeler
Teague
Sinclair

Thompson
Johnson/Jonsin
Boyd
Fillmore/Filmore/Philmore (Philmor)
Hartwill/Hartwell
Meeks/Meaks
Bragg
Fielding
Dempsey/Dempsay
Peas/Pease
Hilliard
Gilford—Gil
Gifford
McDuff—Duff
Littleton
Gowland
Whitfield
Branson
Lawson
Bell
Redding
Whitfield
Branson
Conrad/Konrad—Connie
Murrah
White
Alford (or Alphord)
Bradford   [But did not encounter the nickname Brad in this time period]
Fletcher/Flecher
Smith—Smitty
Truman
York

Byford
Miller
Overton
Plummer
Polkb
Hensley
Nolan/Nollin/Nolin
Wright/Right
Witter [Also Whittier]
Stetson
Drayton
Lockwood
Pembroke
Summerfield
Manlove
Porter
Dillard
Armstrong
Clifford/Cliford
Eldridge/Elbridge
Griffen/Griffin
Dawson
Fleming
Mumford
Foster
Hutton
Hampton
Cullen
Spencer
Henderson
Sanders
Hubbard
DeKalb

Curtis
Talbert
Kemp
Patton/Paton
Harris
Simpson—Simp
Dixon
Quinn
Palmer
Winfield/Windfield—Winnie
Shelby
Decatur
Lockhart/Lockheart   [Nickname "Hart" encountered numerous times]
Posey
Benton—Bent
Thornton—Thorn/Torn
Mason
Shelton
Todd
Gardner
Hudge
Wallace
Reese/Reace
Riley
Ardell
Pitts
Howell—Howie
Pratt
Drury
Crawford/Crofford
Harmon
Avery
Middleton

Morgan—Morg
Hinson
Redman
Quitman
Garland
Preston
Buell
Armistead/Armisted/Armsted/Armstead
Willoughby—Will or Willie
Musgrove

NAMES DERIVED FROM THE ENGLISH LANGUAGE OR CULTURE:

Buck
Money
Dollar
Grand
Friday
Sunday
Marshall
Walter—Walt
Beverley/Beverly
Elmer/Almer
Zeno
Fountain
Culbert—Bert
Mint
Lock
Origin
Authur/Auther/Author[Variation of Arthur?]
Arthur/Author—Artie

Brink
Miner
Lawyer/Law
Cave
Church
Lomax
Marvell
Hay/Hie   [Short for Haywood?]
Pitch   [Pitchfork as a nickname recorded twice]
Gresy   [Noted several times. Was this misspelled form of Greasey?]

Wade
Line
Moles
Morris/Maurice
Adolphus or Adolph—Dolph
Rodolphus/Dolphus—Rudie or Dolph
Alphonso
Cheyne/Cheyney
Greenville
Herbert—Bert   [But did not encounter nickname Herb in this time period]

Cuthbert—Bert
Albert/Albertus—Al or Bert
Lambert—Bert
Bibert—Bert
Ubertus—Bert
Lybertus—Bert
Bartlett/Bertlett—Bart/Bert
Rush
Otto
Basil
Willis

Tolliver/Toliver
Wilford
Moritz
Michael/Mical—Mike
Barclay
Asbury/Ashbury—Ash
Boyce/Boice
Casey
William/Williom—Will or Willie/Willy or Bill or Billy/Billie
Anthony/Antny/Antony/Antonie [But not Tony]
Price
Step
Dudley/Dudly
Angus
Doak
Sandy
Jacob—Jake
Clay
Blake
Jamison/Jemison
Neil/Neill/Neal/Neall
Harvey/Harve/Herve/Hervey
Hockley
Linn/Lynn
Bruno
Bugg
Yancey
Eugene—Gene
Creasey/Creasy/Cresy
Dean/Deen
Fritz—Fritzy
Butch [One of my nicknames growing up in Wyoming. Possibly derived from Butcher, though mine comes from "butch haircut."]

Humphrey—Hump
Felix/Phelix
Etham
Marlen [But not Marlin ....]
Jerry
Clement
Cashaway—Cash
Nicholas/Nicolas—Nick
Dunis [?]
Theodore—Theo or Ted or Ned
Theophilus/Theofilus—Theo
Gipson or Gibson—Gip or Gib
Andre
Drew
Wyatt/Wiatt/Wyat
Sealey
Gasper/Gaspur
Sylvester/Silvester
Thirsten
Flavius
Wenzel
Bernhard/Bernhardt
Edward—Ed/Edd or Eddie/Eddy/Edy or Ned
Claiborne/Claiborn/Clayborn/Clayburn/Claibourn—Clay or Clabe
Cecil
Ira
Emil
Alonso—Lon
Francis—Frank or Frankie
Innis
Leroy/LeRoy—Roy
Floyd/Floid
Charles—Charlie/Charley/Charly or Chuck

Herf/Herff
Boss/Bose
Ora
Barney
Lorenzo—Lo
Elmo
Leonard—Leo
Hatch
Milburn/Milborn
Hugh/Hue
Jesse—Jess (Jese)
Lester—Les
Burrell—Burl/Berl
Burl/Burley/Berly/Birl
Marion
Otis
Lloyd/Loyd
Tyre [Pronounced Tie-Ree]
Ross
Shadle
Clifton
Louis/Lewis—Lou
Calvin—Cal
Alfred—Alf or Fred
Milton—Milt
Arba
Ozius
Oliver—Ollie
Perry
Victor
Pierce/Pearce
Phineas/Fineas
Ira

Festus
Clay
George—Georgie
Chester
Clarence/Clarance
Claude
Dexter—Dex
Francis
Lamar
Lee
Malcolm
Zane
Stanley—Stan
Mahlon—Lon
Martin—Mart
Raymond—Ray
Hamilton—Ham
Pinkney/Pinkny—Pink
Brice/Bryce
Gotcha/Gotchea   [Not a nickname either!]
Biscoe
Jepe/Jepie
Dennis/Denis   [Yippee! Actually, Dennis was as uncommon then as now. Its high point, for Baby Boomers like me, was a result of an infamous comic strip, which I have never lived down. The Spanish versions, Dionysio and Dionisio, were more common in the Old West than the English spelling. I didn't run across the nicknames Den or Denny in this time period.]
Cumberland
Stoke
Archibald—Archie or Arch or Archy
Donie [Possibly a nickname for Donald]

Brantley
Wade
Gasaway
Mannax
Alexander—Alec/Aleck or Alex/Elex or Ellic/Elic (Elexander—Ellick)
Ellic/Elic
Mingo
Buto
Haywood/Heywood—Wood or Woody/Woodie
Bibb   [Possibly a nickname]
Sulner
Orin (Orren)
Pasqual/Pascual/Pascale
Artimis/Artemis/Artimus
Larkin
Randall/Randal/Randle—Randy
Conrad
Sebastian/Sebastien
Sudduth/Suddeth—Suddy
Simms/Sims
Isadore
Quince
Tamar/Tamer
Lawrence/Larence/ Lorence   [But did not see "Larry" in this time period]
Monroe/Munro/Monro/Manroe/Munroe
Haywort
Noble
Owen (Owin)
Triphon
Thaddeus/Thadeus/Thadues—Thad or Tad
Reinhart
Burgess/Burgiss/Burgis
Bazel

Nash
Trangott   [What an ugly name, but encountered numerous times during research]
Holland
Tobias—Tobe/Tobey
Ambrose/Amrose
Heber
Hardie
Jasper
Droudy/Drowdy
Sidney/Sidny—Sid
Dudley/Dudly—Dud
Dover
Brown
Mahew/Mahue
Grady
Giles/Jiles
Milo/Mylo
Wesley/Wessly/Westly—Wes
Christopher/Christofer/Christerfer/Christerpher (Christoph)—Chris
Champman
Littleberry
Wiley
Joshaway/Josaway—Josh
Moss
Rhett/Rett/Rit
Parky
Josie/Jossee
Bock
Barnabas
Mitchell—Mich
Spartan
Zachariah—Zach/Zack

Bartley/Bartly
Cederus
Dates
Armand
Zaccheus
Zeke
Banner
Simp/Sim
Shadick—Shad
Harrison/Harison
Elwin
Erasmus
Gaston
Alphes
Wylie
Harry/Hary [Not always from "Harold"]
Prior/Prier
Amanger
Murdoch/Murdoc/Murdock/Meurdoch—Dock/Doc
Norman
Edmund/Edmond/Edman
Brister/Bristo
Sanford/Sandford
Bowden
Hardeman/Hardiman
Sherrod
Bufford/Buford
Cap [Probably a nickname]
Handy
Please
Hamish/Hamlish/Hemlish/Hemilish
Lowery/Lowry
Platt

Prospect
Ransom/Ransome
Whiton/Whinton—Whit
Whetstone—Stony
Ewing
Junio/Junie
Coleman/Colman
Newell/Newley
Cordell—Cord—Del
Granbury/Granberry
Kit   [Also a nickname, short for Christopher]
Rice
Champion—Champ
Dougal/Dugal
Malone—Mal
Macon
Seeley/Seely
Holly/Hollie   [Also widely used as a nickname.]
Tay
Dunk/Dunking   [Quite a few instances, and it appears to have been a formal name, not a nickname]

BLACK MEN'S NAMES

Black names during the slave period tended to be the same as or similar to white names. After Emancipation and through the Old West period, there seems to have been little variation. This is not so today. The names listed here are noteworthy for the time period.

Amsiah
Denzil/Densil
Galille
GenGen   [Unsure of the pronunciation, whether it's jen-jen or gen-gen]

Gideon/Gidian
Jams/Jamsuh/Jam/Jamms
Jopee
Kinchen
Osca   [A variation of Oscar?]
Pampie   [A variation of Pompie?]
Pleaston   [A variant of Pleasanton?]
Porry
Poto
Rendy
Rolley/Roley
Silla/Sillah
St. Peter
Sylvesta   [A variant of Sylvester]
Thed
Tishus
Letsy

HISPANIC MEN'S NAMES
Author's Favorite: Dionysio (of course...!)

Note: Today, as then, the migration routes from Mexico are fairly defined. The Gulf states and central Mexico (Chihuahua east) are what I term the eastern corridor into Texas, and the western corridor (Sonora west) into Arizona and California. The differences in names are very important, and I leave it to a Mexican historian to sort out.]

CALIFORNIA/ARIZONA

Brigidio
Alvion
Christofero

Chalo
Florentino
Cleovaro
Levio
Danacio [Dionisio? One can only hope ….]
Mequie
Dilda
Nestor
Pascal/Pascual
Sabino
Silvero
Trancito
Ygenio/Ygencio
Puto [Encountered this more than once … as a given name, not a nickname]

Vicento
Emil
Calistro/Calistre/Calistoro/Calstro
Niconar
Alcario
Cirraco
Calixto
Sostenes/Sosthenes ["Toss the Knees" encountered once. An Anglicanization.]

Abalos/Abalo
Baisa/Bisa
Chopito
Levitas
Librado [Also a woman's name Librada]
Telesfor/Teleflor
Sacarellas
Frackario
Ygenio
Meregildo

Ambrosio
Libredo
Noverto
Dubiger/Dubiguer

NEW MEXICO

Canuto
Trinidad
Andres
Cornelio
Florian
Petro
Lauro
Conrado
Vicanor
Cayetano/Gayetano/Kiatano
Demetrio
Elisio/Eliso
Abdenago
Geronimo   [Pronounced Hair-on-i-mo or Hee-ran-ee-moh]. Only in English is this Jer-on-ih-moh]]
Celestino
Patrocino
Albino
Terminio
Ultimio/Ultimo/Ultimus
Cecilio
Romero
Celso
Secundino/Secundo
Corpio

Blas   [Prononced Blah]
Hilario   [Prononced Il-ar-io]
Melchor
Masedonio
Severo
Desidero/Desiderio
Dario
Serapio
Psenini
Ciseroe
Elchor
Victoriano

TEXAS

Jorge
Elizario
Correlio
Cornelio
Felipe
Carlos
Pedro
Francisco
Gabriel
Gordo   [Mostly see this as a nickname, meaning "fat," but possibly used as a name, too.]
Jose
Estamatado/Estimado
Eusebio
Segundo
Guillermo   [William in English]
Manuel

Candelario
Honorio
Jesus
Porfirio
Anastacio
Prudencio
Miguel/Maguel
Juan
Fabio
Teodoro   [Also Teodora for women]
Pancho
Canuto
Ramon
Chico
Santiago
Eulogio
Gregorio
Sancho   [Interesting history to this. In Spanish literature, Sancho Panza, of course, was Don Quixote's sidekick. Today, many Hispanics use it to describe a secret boyfriend—or "sancha" in the case of a secret girlfriend!]
Romaldo
Raymundo
Nicanor
Laureano
Serveriano/Severio
Eulalio/Ulalio
Pero
Profito
Macario
Fermin/Fermine
Nestor

Domingo
Modesto

MEN'S NICKNAMES

Author's Favorite: Slippery   [Hence the title of this book *Slippery Jack*]

Note: Nicknames associated with common given names, such as Jack for John, Dick for Richard, and Jim for James, are not listed here.

NAMES DERIVED FROM PLACES:

Glasgow
Yankee/Yank
Misourie/Missouri
Laramie/Laramy
Indiana
North
Texas—Tex   [Most often a nickname, but occasionally encountered as a name]
Troy
Tennessee
Pedernales/Perdinales/Pertinallis/Pertenallis
San Jacinto
Orleans
Luss
Carlisle
Danish
Alabama
Laramie/La Ramie
Idaho

Ireland
Alabaman
Arkansas
California
Alabama
Texas—Tex
Long Tex
Big Tex
Little Texas
Colorado
Florida
Arizona
Montana
Missouri/Missourie
Arkansas
Idaho
Mexican
Cimmaron
Pecos
Sabine
Purgatoire   [Often pronounced "Picketwire']
Cascade
Sierra
Rocky/Rockie
Rocky Mountain
Roseburg/Roseberg
Yakima
Ranier
Butte
Pocatello
Boise
Sawtooth
Bozeman
Missoula

Tularosa/Tulorosa
Socorro/Socoro
Santa Fe/Santo Fe/Santafe
Rincon
Colfax
Eddy
Brazos
Gila
Nogales
Saguaro   [Also Sahuaro]
Maricopa
Prescott/Prescote
Sidona   [Encountered five times, but modern spelling Sedona, never]
Nueces   [New Aces—Probably a spelling mistake, but a fun nickname, nonetheless]

NAMES DERIVED FROM CHARACTERISTICS:

Smart
Lucky
Sullen
Iron
Trusty
Hindsight
Spunk
Honest
Old
Young
Papa/Pappy
Uncle (Unc)
Jawbone   [One individual researched also used the initials "J.B." It's unclear whether J.B. comes from a nickname—Jawbone— or whether Jawbone was a formal name and J.B. was the nickname!]

Bone/Boney/Bony
Hambone
Swine   [Swin encountered twice. "Pig" never, but Piggie twice]
Rowdy   [Roudie encountered once]
Bloody
Long-Haired
Dirty
Son
"Big Daddy"
Cripple/Crip
Nine-Finger
One-Eye
Stoke
Rebe
Rebell/Rebel
Mingo
Bose
Driver
Tamer
Dollar
Salt Lick
Dug
Danish
Fudge   [A name and a nickname]
Bib
Ebb
Oat/Oats
Crossways
Hop
Jump
"Bubba"
Betcha
Crash

SLIPPERY JACK

Bumple
Dub
Tip
Ding
Pie
Dixie
Ag
Aug/Augie
Smiley
Poke
Concho
Stonewall/Stonewal [Probably derived from Stonewall Jackson, post Civil War]
Bat [Not always derived from Bartholomew]
Bent
Leather
Ruff & Ready
Bird
Black
Red
Moonlight
Onions
Pepper
Salty
Stitch
Calm
Parge
Puss
Pick
Pony
Smiley
Champ
Brick
Gee

41

Bummer
Chick
Grude   [short for Magruder?]
Powder   [Gunpowder encountered only once]
Flash
Creek
Butcher/Butch
Stubborn
Steady
Ready
Doubtful/Doubting
Worthy
Punk   [Probably from fire-making rather than the modern connotation]
Sad
Smoky/Smokey
Poor
Deaf
Dumb   [Perhaps "mute," in the modern sense, perhaps not ....]
Blind
Cripple
Free
Stingy
Salty
Quick
Fat
Old
Young
Big
Little
Yellow
Blue
Loyal
Wild

Right
Lawless   [Encountered only twice, breaking my rule of 5, but so good I'm including it anyway.]

FAMOUS MEN'S NICKNAMES
Author's Favorite: "Yellowstone" Kelly   Luther S. Kelly

Note: In most cases, I combined formal names with nicknames. In fact, however, contemporaries probably didn't know these individuals' formal names and called them only by their nicknames and aliases. Because of that, go through this list and read the nicknames and last names to get a feel for the people in their time. Example, "Black Face" Bryant rather than Charles Bryant.

"Black Face Charlie" or "Black Face" Charles Bryant
"Lucky" Baldwin or Elias J. Baldwin
"Long-Haired Jim" Timothy Courtright
"Lotly cooler" Charlie Crawford
"Pony" Charles Ray Diehl
"The Prowler" Caleb Hall
"Turkey Creek" Jack Johnson
"Ranger" Jones [an outlaw]
"Canada Bill" William Jones
"Cherokee Bill" William Kellam
"Cowboy Bill" William King
"Cock-eyed" Frank Loving
"Rowdy Joe" Joseph Lowe
"Gunplay" Clarence Maxwell or James Otis Bliss
"Happy Jack" John Morco
"Killing Jim" James Brown Miller, aka: "Killer" Miller and "Deacon" Jim
"Big Indian" Robert Olinger aka: Pecos Bob
"Texas Jack," John Baker Omohundro   [Lots of "Texas Jacks" in the era]

"Johnny-Behind-the-Deuce" John O'Rourke
"Doboy" Phillip Goodbread Taylor   [Sometimes seen as "Doughboy," a name derived from his mother's maiden name, Goodbread]
"Texas Billy" William Thompson
"Shoot-Your-Eye-Out" John Wilson Vermillion   [aka: another "Texas Jack"]
"Big Time Charlie" Charles Allen
"The Fixer" Lou Blonger   [aka: Louis Blonger]
"Swiftwater" William Bill Gates   [Not the computer guy ....]
"Umbrella Jim" James Miner
"Soapy" Smith, Jefferson Randolph Smith
"Lucky Bill" William B. Thornton [Gambler]
"Poker Bill" William Thornton   [New Mexico Territorial Governor]
"Yellow Kid" Joseph Weil
"Red Jack" Almer Jack Averill
"Bronco Bill," William E. Walters
"Rattlesnake Dick," Richard Barter
"Clay," Robert A. Allison
"Nubbin's Colt," Seaborn Barnes
"Old Man" Newman Haynes Clanton
"Bitter Creek" George Newcomb
"Nigger General" Samuel Fields, aka Sly-Coon or General Darkey [A well known Deadwood character that didn't seem to mind racist references to his color.]
"Deadwood Dick" Nat Love
"Wobblin' Willie" Balleau
"Sport" Boyle
"Buffalo Bill" William A Brooks   [One of many "Buffalo Bills" including William F. Cody]
"Long-haired Sam" Brown
George Francis "Big-Nose George" Curry aka: George Manuse, George Curry, or Big Nose George or Flat Nose
"Texas" John Slaughter
"HooDoo Brown" Hyman G. Neill

SLIPPERY JACK

"Red Buck" George Weightman
"Cherokee Bill" Crawford Goldsby
"Black Jack" Thomas Edward Ketchum
"Clubfoot" George Lane
"Red" Erastus Yager
"Buckskin" Frank Leslie or "Buckskin Frank", Nashville Franklyn Leslie
"Kid Curry" Harvey Alexander Logan

"Wild Bill"	William Preston Longley [Known after death as "Bloody Bill"]
"Wild Bill"	James Butler Hickok
"Wild Charlie"	Nathaniel E. Wyatt aka: "Zip" Wyatt
"Rattlin Bill"	
"Big Steve" Lory	
"Mysterious Dave"	David Allen Mather
"Pegleg" Eldridge	
"Dirty Dave" Rudabaugh	
"Catch 'Em Alive Jack	John Abernathy [1876-1941]
"American Horse"	Wasechun-tashunka
"Brown" Bowen	Joshua Robert Bowen [1849-1878]
"Windy" or "Frank"	Francis P. Cahill [killed by Billy the Kid, 1877]
"Bat" Masterson	
"Mannen" Clements	Emmanuel Clements, Sr.[1845-1887]
"Mannie" Clements	Emmanuel Clements, Jr. [1868-1908]
"Simp" Dixon	Simpson Dixon
"Lame Johnny"	Cornelius Donahue [hanged in 1878]
"Billy Profane"	William B. Fain
"Louis A. McLaughlin"	Elijah Gilbert
"Add" Jones	Addison Jones [African American cowboy]
"Nigger Jim" Kelly	James Kelly [African American wrangler]
"Stuttering Bob"	Robert Lewis
"Jim Talbott"	James Sherman
"Bear George"	George B. McClellan

"Fat Mac"	William McKee
"Bass Outlaw/Baz Outlaw"	Basil Outlaw, a lawman
June Peak	Junius Peak
"Uncle Jack Robinson"	John Robertson
"Frenchy Rochas"	Francois Jean Rochas
"Sul" Ross	Lawrence Sullivan Ross, namesake of Sul Ross University, president of Texas A&M University, and a Confederate general
"Pete" Spence or Elliot Larkin/"Lark" Ferguson	Peter Spencer
"Father Van"	William Westley Van Orsdel
"Wylackie John"	John D. Wathen
"Three-Legged Willie"	Robert McAlpin Williamson
"One-Armed Johnny"	John Logan
"Bummer Dan"	Daniel McFadden
"Teddy Blue"	E.C. Abbott
'Canada Bill"	William Jones
"Daddy"	Peter P. Ackley
"Broncho John"	John Sullivan
"Doc"	J.M. Day
"Print"	Isom Prentice Olive
"Bill"	William Brocious
"Joe Horner"	Frank Canton
"Sug" Cummings	
"Green" Denson	John M. Denson
"Three-Fingered Jack"	Jack Dunlap or W.H. Lausteneau
"Border Boss"	John R. Hughes
"Kid"	Elmer Lewis
"Bravo Juan"	Juan Yoas
"Cash"	Cassius Hollister
"Hard Luck"	Rollie Harrison
"Hurricane Bill"	William A. Martin
"Little Dick" West	Richard West

SLIPPERY JACK

"Bad Land Charlie"	Charles Anderson
"Tallow Man" Crosby	Harry Crosby
"Dangerous Dick the Terrapin"	Dick Davis
"Persimmon Bill"	
"Brown"	
"Tobacco Jake"	
"Push" Folsom	Johnson Fulsom
"Pretty Boy"	Frank Wallace
"Billy the Kid"	William H. Bonney
"English Jack"	John Curry
"Big Nose" Kate	Kate Elder
"Big Bill"	William C. Gilson
"Comanche Jim"	James W. Grahame
"Whiskey Jim"	Jack Greathouse
"Little Arkansas"	John Wesley Hardin [A nickname Hardin recalled in his autobiography. Whether anyone *else* called him by this name or the nickname "Seven-up" is debatable.]
"Hard Times"	"Doc" Hearn
"Kansas Bill"	
"Cheap John"	John Marks
"Hurricane Bill"	William A. Martin
"Bat" Masterson	William Barclay Masterson
"Hi" Millett	Hiram Millett
"Monte Jack"	
"Phin" Reynolds"	Phineas W. Reynolds
"Old John" or "Uncle John"	John Selman, Sr.
"Young John" or "Marion"	John Selman, Jr.
"One-Arm Bill"	William J. Wilson
"Three-Legged Willie"	Judge Robert McAlpin Williamson
"Canada Bill"	William Jones
"X"	John Xavier Beidler

"Monte Frank"	Frank Boyd
"Slim Jim" Bruce	James Bruce
"El Dorado Johnny"	John Dennis
"Willy Hicky" or "Hicker"	James Fulsom
"Grasshopper Sam"	
"The Handsome Kid"	
"Off-Wheeler"	J.J. Harlan
"Kit" Carson	Christopher Houston Carson
"Outlaw Bill" Moore	W. C. Moore
"Deadshot"	William Moss
"Nut Shell Bill"	
"Pancho" or "Francisco Villa"	José Doroteo Aranga Arambula
"O. Henry"	William Sydney Porter
"Little Bill"	William F./ Raidler
"Mark Twain"	Samuel Langhorne Clements [My grandmother's grand uncle!]
"Bear River Tom"	Thomas J. Smith
"Haw"	H.A.W. Tabor
"Tomcat"	Thomas Selman
"Little Rick"	Dick West
"Yellowstone Kelly"	Luther S. Kelly
"Tallow Man"	Harry Crosby
"Kid Curry"	Harvey Logan
"Sundance Kid"	Harry Alonzo Longabaugh
"Persimmon Bill"	William Chambers
"Bad Land Charlie"	Charles Anderson
"Cock-Eyed Frank"	Frank Loving
"Broncho Billy"	G. M. Anderson
"Bloody Bill"	William Anderson
"Trick"	Brown
"Buffalo Bill"	William F. Cody
"Baldy Russell"	William Mitchell
"Happy Jack"	John Morco

"Butch" Cassidy   George Leroy Parker
"Pony" Reid
"Apache Bill"   William Semans
"Sombrero Jack"   George Shaffer
"Rackety"   Erastus Smith
"Barney O'Tool"   Charles Williams
"Cheap John"   John Marks
"Laramie Dan"   Dan Moran
"Chalk"   Chalkey McArtor Beeson
"French Creek" Ben Wheeler   William Robinson
John "Crooked Mouth" Green
William Frank "Doc" Carver (Called "The Evil Spirit of the Plains" by the
    St. Louis Republican newspaper)
James "Jim Kid" Willoughby
Buck "King of the Cowboys" Taylor
Delbert C. "Bush Bill" Clement
Lucien Bonaparte Maxwell, "Boss of the Cimarron"
Richard "Dixie Lee" Gray
"Red Buck" Waightman
George "Hookey" Miller
"Russian Bill" William R. Tettenborn
Ollie "Heavy" Lancaster
"Rattlesnake Dick" Barter [also "The Pirate of the Placers"]
William "Hunkdory" Holmes
"Three-Fingered" Jack
"Dynamite Bill"
"Arkansas Tom Jones" Roy Daugherty
"HooDoo Brown" H.G. Neill
John "Little Allen" Llewellyn [There are several other Llewelyns in the Old
    West called "Little Allen"
Charles "Black Bart" Boles
James Addison Reavis "James Addison Peraltareavis "Baron of Arizona"
"Cactus Jack"   John Nance Garner

MISCELLANEOUS:

Bar
Bush
Linder
Freeman/Freman
Clemons
Romain
Payton/Peyton
Patrick/Patric—Paddy   [Not just an Irish name.]
Walton—Walt
Ashford
Hardy
Parham/Parchman
Upton
Roux
Jarrel/Jarrell
Kinian
Alden
Stitch   [Also a nickname]
Miles
Darling   [A formal name]
Lemons
Drumann/Druman
Rowan
Tench   [A nickname?]
Coley
Durkee
Heck   [Heck Thomas, for example]
Hunter
Richmond/Richman—Rich
Schuyler
Chesley

SLIPPERY JACK

Trampas [From the Spanish *tramposo*, a cheater. A memorable rustler in Owen Wister's iconic novel, *The Virginian*.]
Jerry/Gerry/Jerey
Ebb
Kincher—Kinch
Kinchin—Kinch
Kinchion—Kinch
Christian/Krischeon—Chris/Kris
Archelaus
Parlee/Parley—Lee [Similar to the woman's name Parilee]
Lane
Hamlin—Ham
Ephrin
Presley [But no Elvis noted in this time period.]
Rusk
Calvert/Colvert
Dobson—Dob
Millard
Oneal [No apostrophe]
Neal/Neel
Selden
Marsh
Primus
Sterling
Murray
Jarvis/Gervis
Ney
Vander
Duff
Roderick/Rodrick—Roddy [Possibly the nickname Rowdy, too]
Feriby/Feribee
Graves
Rudolph—Rudy/Rudie

Frey
Mortimer—Mort
Roscoe/Rosco
Eustis—Stacy
Beauford/Beafort/Beuford/Beauforth—Beau
Tuckin
Fox
Barclay/Barcley
Hellmutt—Mutt
Hansell
Godfrey/Godfray
Patch   [Also a nickname]
Prewitt
Ling   [A nickname?]
Sellars
Rankin
Crispin
Bass/Baz
Britton
Javin/Gavin
Tiskey
Wisgey
Whiskey/Whisky   [Wisky encountered only once]
Sol   [Also a nickname]
Argalus
Bayless
Bluford
Bristoe
Broadus
Burwell/Burewill
Burk
Carey—Cary
Gabril

52

Catchings—Kitch/Catch
Ladd—Laddie/Laddy
Landrum—Land
Larry/Larey
Llewellyn
Sid
Wayte—Wait/Wate
Caspar/Casper
Obal
Birdwell—Bird
Coke
Manley
Sylvan/Sylvanus
Lockey
Dandridge—Dandy
Irvin/Ervin
Florian
Osso
Frebank/Freebank (Freebanck)
Cussey
Hain
Clyde/Clide
Strother   [example Strother Martin, actor, though after this time period]
Gunton
Derrick/Derek
Jonathan/Johnathan—John or Johnny
Dug   [A name and a nickname]
Alves
Add   [A nickname, for sure, but likely a formal first name too.]
Grenville/Granville
Hyman/Himan

Esack [variation of Isaac]
Dunkin
Wallace/Walice
Deveray/Devreay
Ambro
Abert
Gift
Dieter/Deter [Usually a Germanic, or ethnic name, but sometimes encountered with surnames of English derivation]
Currier
Rare [A rare name ....]
Piedmont/Piedmon
Spyers
Morcline
Hilder
Dublin—Dub
Gersham
Byars
Neibhur
Farrel
Derry
Lemlow
Tan
Bendy
Chauncey/Chuncey
Belo
Mise
Conley/Counlee/Counley/Connally
Flornoy
Appleton
Ferren/Ferrin
Manning
Bootley

Leonider
Risam
Albet
Sopher
Bursh
Bazaine
Calyer
Greer
Morgue
Poke
Clouds
Saberry
Guy/Guye
Killady
Argyle/Argyly
Beech
Bier
Cupples
Marshal/Marshall
Muggin
Ovid
Shaw
Halelton
Sep
Derrell/Darel/Darrell
Sambo [Traditionally meant "second son," but quickly lost that meaning as it was used for any sons. And, contrary to what one might think, doesn't seem to be identified with any particular race, at least through the 1880s.]
Nye
Harley
Besford
Waldo

Zoe
Delbert
Dimarous
Delfino
Afton
LaRue
Sully
Theophilas
Irby
Ninnian
Derwood/Durwood
Alvro
Verble/Verbel
Beck
Albany
Branch
Shipton—Ship
Thadius
Nistar
Tellman
Theron
Fergis/ Furgus
Orlando
Alanson
Pass
Perdy
Morey
Boulden
Theadore
Anslum
Allis
Hilery
Alpheus

Micujah
Irving
Jewell
Mancell
Lanham
Bink
Mabry
Hurschell
Ozeeley
Brock
Bolliver
Altamont
Blevins
Sherrill
Halcut
Tally
Alten
Collander
Puckett
Fortas
Bee
Olander
Lace
Cade
Chesterfield
Lew/Lou
Wilst/Whilst
Mortimer/Mortamore
Achabonz/Achabons
Westleu
Borrum
Bock
Sebellin/Sebeln--Seb

Tellis
Tiliwines
Cambell
Hall/Haul
Dink/Dinky
Singleton
Boland
Sipp
Toney
Paschal
Shug
Asah/Asa
Payne
Acey
Dempsey/Dempsay-Dems/demp
Zilpher
Colum
Pitt
Cheyny/Cheney
Spurgeon
Grier
Granville
Larke
Sol
Anders
Marsen
Dandridge
Manderville
Collin
Colum
Scrap
Rowland
Allberry

Lynard
Orith
Rufus/Ruffis—Rufe
Cletus
Frits
Hurly
Tenly
Crittenton/Crittendon-Crit
Forman
Lachlan
Curry
Morean
Ambros
Furnell
Brice
Armand
Cane
Comer
Monte

WOMEN'S GIVEN NAMES

Author's Favorite: **K'turah** [K'turah Watts, my grandaunt's name, though she died a long time before I was born.]

Note: a Southern variant Miss + Name as in: Miss Sally, Miss Martha, or Miss Rose. A middle name variant with names like Mae and Lou as in Sally Mae, Cleta Mae, Betty Lou, or Elsie Lou, plus, a Catholic variant Sister + name as in Sister Mary Ann, Sister Rose, etc.

Also, unlike men of this time period, women did not seem to use their initials to identify themselves. An example is with two research interests of mine—W.C. Williams and his daughter Helen Beulah Mrose—only the father went by his initials.

Other names were often used in combinations, such as Belle, Jane, Rita, Mary, Ellen, or Lou. My grandmother was Mary Ellen Watts.

Finally, there are many examples of combination names like Maryann, Lucyjane, or Mayrose.

NAMES DERIVED FROM CHARACTERISTICS:

Grace
Temperance—Temp or Tempa or Tempe/Tempie/Tempy/Tempey
Patience
Nice
Charity/Cherity
Euphoria
Golden
Golda
Amity
Dearie
Unity
Honey
Desire
Polite
Love or Lovey
Even
Noble
Promise
Freedom
Hope
Thrift
Welcome
Dimple
Icy Lee
Faith
Nicety
Mourning
Friend
Constance/Constants
Piety
Felicity
Dancer

Prudence/Prudens—Prudie
Idea
Person
Self
Libertine   [Strange name to be saddled with…]
Saluda   [Possibly a Texas variant of the Spanish "salud," or health]
Right
Willowy
Welcome

NAMES DERIVED FROM HISTORY, LITERATURE, OR THE BIBLE:

Cleopatra/Cleapatra/Cleapatria—Cleo
Penelope—Penny or Nell/Nel
Esmerelda/Esmeralda
Venus/Venis
Vesta
Beulah/Beula (Bulah)   [Means "married" in Hebrew]
Salome/Saloma
Salomine
Empress
Pocahantas
Electra

NAMES DERIVED FROM STONES/PRECIOUS STONES:

Ruby/Rubye/Rhube   [On a personal note, three of the author's relatives through his paternal grandmother were Opal, Ruby, and Pearl. Similar "groupings" were used in other families.]

Pearl—Pearly/Pearlie
Jewel/Jewell
Jade
Tapaz/Topas
Safire/Saphire/Sapphire
Opal/Obal
Garnet/Garnete
Lapis
Beryl/Beril
Agat   [I assume this was "Agate." Observed five times, same spelling.]

Moonstone   [Unsure if this was a formal name or a nickname.]
Jaspera/Jasperah
Beryl/Beril   [Also Berylee]
Coral/Korral   [Encountered Coralee twice]
Amber
Amethyst
Emerald
Beryl
Petra

NAMES DERIVED FROM PLACES:

Georgia
Dixie
California
Sedona/Sidona or Sidoney/Sidonie
Tennessee/Tenissee—Tenne
Kentucky
America (Merica)
Columbia

Texana/Texanna/Texannah/Texana or Texann or Texas   [The name Texana was very popular.]
Tehanna/Tejana   [from the Spanish pronunciation of Texana]
East Texas
Arizona—Zona
Nevada
Indiana/Indianna/Indiannah
Refugia   [An Irish colony in the Mexican Province of Tejas was centered on a mission at Refugio, pronounced in Spanish as Reh-FU-hio. Whether the Irish mispronounced it or later Anglo settlers doesn't matter, but many modern "gringos" (including the author) in Texas pronounce it reh-FUR-ee-oh. In this time period the correct pronunciation of the female name was probably Reh-FUR-ee-ah.]
Florida/Floridah
Missouri/Missouria/Missuri/Missoury/Misourie/ Missourey or Misuary/Mosouri
Louisianna/Louisianah/Louisana
Louisanna   [Probably a combination of two names, rather than a state name]
Fredonia/Fredona   [Commonly used in Texas, after the Fredonia Rebellion]
Santafe/Santa Fe
Mississippi
Alabama
Abilene/Abiline/Abeline   [The first two spellings pronounced AB-ah-leen; the last AB-ah-lin or Ab-ah-leen.]
Virginia
Pennsylvania
Sonora/Sonoria—Nora
Palestine/Pollestine
Italla

Tunis
Frenchie
Cuba
Bunivista [The Spanish is "Buena Vista," pronounced bwenah veestah, but in Colorado, the town's name, and this woman's name, is boon ah vistah]

NAMES DERIVED FROM FLOWERS:

Rose or Rosy/Rosie
Iris
Daisy
Petunia
Geranium [Or Geri}
Violet/Violett or Viola
Hyacinth [Hiasinth encountered once]
Oleander
Columbine/Colombine
Daphne/Dafney
Gladys/Gladis
Olive/Olivia
Peony
Fern
Lily
Bloom [Encountered only twice]
Pansy
Rose
Rosemary [Of course, may also be derived from Rose + Mary]
Petunia/Patunia
Tulip/Tulipe

Amaryllis/Amaryllus/Amarillah/Amarilla   [The last may be a Spanish variant, therefore pronounced am-a-ree-yah]
Dahlia/Dallia

COMMON WOMEN'S NAMES

Aba
Abbie
Abby
Abidah
Abigail
Abilene
Abiline
Ada
Adah
Adda
Addie
Addy
Adelaide
Adeline
Adella
Adena
Adline
Agnes
Agnis
Ailsy
Alabama
Albertine
Alice
Aline

Alis
Allice
Alma
Almidy
Almira
Alonetta
Alonettah
Alonette
Alpha
Alsey
Alsie
Althea
Althena
Alva
Alvah
Alzira
Amanda
Amber
Ambrosia
Amelia
America
Amey
Amoretta
Ampy
Amsi
Amy
Ana
Anastacia
Anastasia
Anatha
Andra
Angela
Angie
Anica

Anna
Annah
Annaline
Annie
Antoinette
Antonette
April
Aquilla
Ara
Arabell
Arabella
Araminta
Aranda
Arcada
Ardell
Ardella
Arena
Arinda
Arizona
Arletta
Armanda
Arminta
Arominta
Arrena
Arrenia
Arrie
Artemissa
Artha
Arthesa
Artimisa
Artimisa
Asca
Atelia
Augusta

Aura
Ava
Avah
Babe
Baby
Barah
Barsheba
Bathsheba
Bea
Beatrice
Becca
Becka
Becky
Belinda
Belle
Bernia
Berta
Berth
Bertha
Berthine
Bertie
Bess
Bessie
Bet
Beth
Bethana
Bethanna
Bethannah
Bethany
Bethie
Betsy
Bettie
Betty

Beula
Beulah
Beverley
Beverly
Biddy
Billie
Billie
Biola
Bird
Birdie
Birdy
Bittie
Bitty
Blanch
Blanche
Bridey
Bridgett
Bridgid
Brigette
Brigid
Brigit
Bulah
Caledonia
California
Callie
Cally
Camile
Candace
Candis
Candise
Candy
Carinda
Carla

Caroline
Carrie
Carry
Cary
Casina
Cassandra
Casse
Cassie
Catarina
Cate
Caterina
Catherine
Cathren
Cathrine
Cecilia
Celestin
Celia
Cellie
Cerena
Cesaria
Charity
Charlot
Charlotte
Charlottee
Cheaba
Cheba
Cherity
Cherry
China
Chipita
Cilia
Cilla
Cinah

Cinda
Cintha
Cinthia
Claire
Clara
Clarah
Clare
Clarinda
Clarindah
Clarissa
Clementina
Clementine
Cleo
Cleopatra
Clerissa
Coleen
Colleen
Columbia
Comelia
Constance
Constants
Cora
Corah
Cordelia
Corilla
Correlia
Cortney
Cridia
Crochet
Cyna
Cynthia
Dafney
Daisy

Daphne
Darcus
Darkus
Dathney
Dathula
Dee
Del
Delila
Delilah
Delilia
Dell
Della
Delores
Deloris
Delphi
Denia
Denneth
Desdemona
Desdemore
Desire
Dimetreas
Dimetress
Dimetrias
Dina
Dinah
Dinnah
Dixie
Docia
Dolly
Dones
Dora
Dorah
Dorathea

Dorcas
Dorinda
Dorkus
Dorotea
Dorothea
Dorree
Dosia
Dosiah
Dove
Dru
Drucila
Drucilla
Drucille
Dulcenia
Dunsie
Easter
Eddith
Edison
Edith
Effa
Effie
Ela
Eleanor
Elinor
Eliza
Elizabeth
Ella
Ellen
Ellie
Ellin
Ellisabeth
Elmira
Elmirah

Eloisa
Elsa
Elsie
Elsy
Elvina
Elvira
Elvirah
Em
Emaline
Emasee
Emelie
Emely
Emilia
Emily
Emma
Emmaline
Empress
Emzy
Enema
Esmeralda
Esmerelda
Essie
Estalene
Ester
Ethel
Etheldred
Eugenia
Eugenie
Eula
Eulah
Eulalia
Euna
Euphemia

Euphemy
Euphi+A418mia
Euphoria
Euphronia
Eva
Evalina
Evaline
Eveline
Evelyn
Faith
Fanny
Fany
Fay
Faye
Felice
Feliciana
Feraby
Fereby
Feriba
Feribie
Fernandella
Fidella
Fillis
Finette
Flo
Flor
Flora
Floradora
Florance
Florence
Florentina
Florentine
Florenz

Florida
Flossie
Forence
Frances
Francina
Francine
Frankie
Freda
Fredona
Fredonia
Freeda
Freedia
Freedom
Frenchie
Friday
Frieda
Friend
Gale
Genet
Georgeann
Georgeanne
Georgia
Georgieann
Geraldine
Gert
Gertie
Gertrude
Ginger
Ginnie
Ginny
Gladis
Gladys
Grace

Gregoria
Griffa
Gussie
Gusta
Gwynn
Halda
Hallie
Hanna
Hannah
Harriet
Helen
Helena
Helene
Hellen
Helma
Heloise
Hennetta
Henny
Henrie
Henrieta
Henrietta
Hephsibeth
Hester
Hette
Hettie
Hetty
Hibbette
Holly
Honey
Hope
Hoxie
Hulda
Huldah

Huldy
Hyacinth
Hyne
Ida
Idea
Idel
Idelia
Ilisa
Iliza
Ilsy
Ima
Ina
Inah
Indiana
Indianna
Indiannah
Ines
Inesmere
Inez
Ione
Iris
Irma
Isabella
Isedora
Isidor
Isodora
Isodore
Italla
Ivory
Ivy
Izabella
Jabez
Jeanette

Jeba
Jemima
Jemimah
Jenett
Jenette
Jennie
Jennine
Jenny
Jepatha
Jeptha
Jerusha
Jessee
Jessie
Jewel
Jinny
Jocaline
Jodie
Joe
Josefa
Josepha
Josephe
Josephine
Josey
Josie
Juana
Juanita
Judie
Judith
Judithe
Judy
Jules
Julie
Juliett

Juliette
Julina
June
Justa
Justice
Justina
K'turah
Karaline
Kate
Katherine
Kaziah
Keeziah
Kentucky
Kesiah
Ketura
Keturah
Kezia
Keziah
Kinsey
Kinsy
Kinzy
Kisere
Kisseree
Kissiah
Kissy
Kitty
Kizzie
Kizzy
Labora
Lacresha
Lahoma
Lanora
Laoma

Larane
Larisa
Larissa
Lauda
Laura
Laurah
Laurie
Lavania
Lavender
Lavernia
LaVernia
Lavina
Lavinder
Lavinia
Lavora
Lea
Leah
Lean
Leithy
Lela
Lena
Lenita
Lenna
Lenora
Lenora
Lensy
Lenzy
Leodica
Leonora
Lesba
Leslie
Letha
Lethe

Leticia
Letitia
Letty
Libby
Libertine
Liddia
Liddy
Lil
Lilea
Lille
Lillian
Lilly
Lily
Lina
Lindy
Linelle
Linna
Lisa
Lisah
Litha
Livey
Livinia
Livy
Liz
Liza
Lizzie
Lizzy
Lois
Lola
Lolie
Loo
Lora
Loraine

Lorana
Loreena
Lorena
Lorene
Lorenza
Loressa
Lorinda
Lorissa
Lorraine
Lorrie
Lotta
Lotte
Lou
Loucinda
Louisa
Louisana
Louisanna
Louise
Louisia
Louisiana
Louisianah
Louisianna
Louvenia
Love
Lovey
Lu
Lucia
Lucilla
Lucinda
Lucinday
Lucretia
Lucretia
Lucy

Ludie
Lue
Luela
Luella
Lueza
Luisa
Lula
Lulah
Lulu
Lura
Luraine
Lurana
Lurenza
Lurinda
Lurithy
Lurity
Lusena
Lutelia
Lutetia
Lydia
Mabel
Mable
Macedoni
Macedonia
Macedonie
Maddie
Madelline
Madena
Madora
Mae
Mag
Maggie
Mahala

Mairy
Malinda
Malissa
Malissah
Mamie
Manda
Mande
Mandy
Manerly
Manerva
Maranda
Marandah
Mare
Margaret
Margarita
Margeretta
Maria
Mariah
Marianna
Marie
Marietta
Marinda
Marsha
Martha
Martilena
Mary
Maryann
Maryjane
Mat
Mathilda
Matilda
Mattie
Maud

Maude
May
Maybelline
Medora
Medorah
Medoria
Meg
Mela
Meldred
Melia
Melinda
Melisah
Melissa
Melvina
Mena
Meola
Meria
Merida
Meridah
Mettie
Midora
Mila
Mildred
Millia
Millicent
Millie
Milly
Mim
Mimms
Mimsie
Mimzy
Mina
Minerva

Miniah
Minna
Minne
Minta
Mintie
Mirah
Miranda
Miria
Mirie
Mirtle
Mississippi
Missourey
Missouri
Missouria
Missoury
Missuri
Mitty
Modena
Mollie
Molly
Mona
Monday
Mopsie
Mordella
Mordica
Mourning
Mryann
Myra
Myrtle
Nadeen
Nancy
Nannie
Nannita

Naomi
Nara
Narcisa
Narcissa
Narcissary
Narcissis
Nel
Nell
Nellie
Nelly
Nerva
Net
Netta
Neve
Nice
Nina
Noble
Nola
Nora
Nora
Norah
Norcissi
Norma
Novella
Nurcissey
Nyla
Obal
Ofelia
Oleander
Olive
Olivea
Olivia
Olly

Opal
Ophelia
Orenya
Orlena
Orna
Ozilla
Palestine
Palmyra
Pam
Pamela
Pamelia
Paralee
Pareley
Paretania
Parilee
Parlee
Parmelia
Parolee
Parthene
Parthone
Pathra
Patience
Patsey
Patsie
Patsy
Paulina
Pauline
Pearl
Pearly
Peggie
Peggy
Pemelia
Penelope

Penina
Penine
Pennicia
Pennsylvania
Penny
Peomelia
Percila
Pernella
Pernellia
Pernellie
Pernesie
Person
Pertina
Petra
Petrah
Phaeba
Phebe
Pheby
Phedora
Philles
Phillipa
Phillis
Philomena
Philomina
Phoeba
Phoebe
Phoebey
Phoebie
Phyllis
Piety
Pilar
Pillar
Please

Pocahantas
Polite
Polka
Pollestine
Pollie
Polly
Portia
Presha
Priciliann
Pricillianne
Priscilla
Priss
Promise
Prudence
Prudencs
Prudens
Pruella
Prus
Pursy
Puss
Queen
Queentina
Ramona
Rebecca
Refugia
Renta
Rhea
Rhoda
Rhube
Rilla
Roda
Roenna
Romona

Rosalie
Rosalind
Rosalinda
Rosalynd
Rosalynda
Rosanna
Rosannah
Rose
Rosella
Rosetta
Rosie
Rosilin
Rosilyn
Rosina
Rosy
Rowenna
Rowenne
Roxanna
Roxanne
Roxie
Roz
Ruby
Rubye
Ruth
Rutha
Sabra
Sadie
Safroney
Safronia
Safrony
Salena
Salina
Sally

Sally Ann
Saloma
Salome
Salomine
Samantha
Santa Fe
Santafe
Santore
Santoree
Santorey
Saphronia
Sara
Sarah
Sarah Ann
Sarah Jane
Sarah Lee
Sarahann
Sarena
Sarene
Sarilda
Satina
Savana
Savanna
Savannah
Scilla
Scintha
Secilia
Sedona
Sedora
Sela
Selah
Selena
Self

Selia
Selina
Sellah
Selma
Semantha
Semanthy
Sementhe
Sena
Sephronia
Serena
Serene
Serilee
Serina
Sernthneta
Sevela
Sevena
Sharlot
Sharlott
Sheba
Sheelah
Sheila
Sheilah
Sibby
Sidona
Sidoney
Sidonie
Sila
Silv
Silvia
Silvie
Sinah
Sinthia
Sinthy

Sister
Solina
Sonora
Sonoria
Sophia
Sophie
Sophronia
Standhope
Stella
Stena
Suda
Sudie
Surrepta
Susan
Susana
Susanna
Susannah
Susie
Susin
Sussanah
Sussi
Sussie
Suz
Suzanna
Suzy
Suzzie
Sybll
Sylla
Sylva
Sylvia
Sythe
Tabby
Tabitha

Tabusha
Taletha
Talitha
Tallulah
Talula
Tamsey
Tandy
Tehanna
Tejana
Tekla
Temp
Tempa
Tempe
Temperance
Tempie
Temple
Tenne
Tennersa
Tennessee
Tepania
Teresa
Terresa
Tess
Texana
Texanah
Texanna
Texannah
Texas
Theadoshia
Theodora
Theodosia
Thoersa
Thrift

Tilda
Tildah
Tilitha
Timprie
Tina
Tollulah
Tolula
Tooka
Tuesday
Tula
Tulah
Tulia
Twila
Tyra
Ugine
Uginia
Uke
Ulna
Unice
Unity
Uzza
Vandy
Velma
Venis
Venus
Vera
Verah
Verona
Vesta
Victora
Victoria
Vina
Vinah

Vincy
Vinetta
Vinette
Vinnie
Viola
Violah
Violet
Virginia
Visa
Vitriona
Vivian
Vivien
Wherta
Wilda
Wilhamina
Wilhelmina
Winifred
Winnie
Zalma
Zania
Zaphronia
Zela
Zella
Zelma
Zera
Zerah
Zeralda
Zeraldah
Zerelda
Zerilda
Zerreldah
Zilpha

Zilphia
Zilphy
Zilta
Zima
Zintha
Zora
Zuda
Zula

OTHER COMMON WOMEN'S NAMES:

Susan/Sousan (or Susin)—Suzy/Susie/Suzzie/Sussie/Sussi/Suse/Susee (Suz)—Sue
Susannah/Susanna/Sussanah/Susana/Suzanna/Sasanna—Susie or Anna
Mina   [Usually pronounced mine-ah, but sometimes as meen-ah]
Emily/Emely/Emelie/Emly/Emley
Helma
Pemelia—Melia
Parmelia—Melia
Correlia
Phebe/Phoebe/Phoebie/Phoeby/Phoebey/Pheby/Phoeba/Phaeba
Cassandra—Cassie/Casse
Zella
Selena/Selina/Salina/Salena/Salina/Solina
Serina
Bertha/Berta—Berth or Bertie or Bert
Berthine—Bertie or Bert
Caroline/Karaline—Callie/Cally or Dolly
Millicent—Millie or Milly
Linna/Lina
Mildred/Meldred—Millie or Milly

Catherine/Katherine/Cathrine/Cathren—Cath   [I did not encounter today's nickname Cathy/Kathy]
Catarina/Caterina
Juana   [Both Juana and Juanita are common with Hispanic women, but both were common with *gringos* of this time period, too.]
Juanita
Vitriona
PetraPetrah
Savannah/Savanna/Savana
Lilly/Lillie/Lille
Lillian—Lil
Rosina
Zuda
Polly/Pollie
Arrenia/Arena/Arrena
Annaline
Mary/Mairy/Mare
Maria/Mariah/Miria/MeriaMarria or Marie/Mirie   [Same pronunciation Mah-ree-ah]
Maryann/Mryann   [A variant of the two names in common usage: Mary Ann.]
Mariah   [Pronounced Mar-eye-ah]
Maryjane   [A variant of the two names in common usage: Mary Jane.]
Maryann or Marianna
Maryrita
Mirium.Marium
Sarahann
Rebecca—Becky/Becka
Bittie
Jenny/Jennie/Jinny/Jinnie/Jinni or Gennie
Ginny/Ginnie
Kitty
Kizzy/Kizzie

Paretania
Timprie
Sylvia/Silvia/Sylva—Silv/Silvie/Silvey
Labora
Mettie
Geraldine/Geraldina—Dina   [Pronounced Dee-nah]
Dinah/Dina/Dinnah   [Pronounced Deye-nah]
Alice/Alis/Allice/Allise
Minerva/Manerva—Minnie
Queen or Queentina—Queeny/Queenie
Augusta—Gusta/Gussie
Dosia [Pronounced Doh-see-ah]
Judy/Judie
Sarah/Sara/Zerah (or Zera)—Sadie   [common variants: Sarah Jane or Sarah Ann]
Anica
Zintha or Sintha
Ruth or Rutha
Amy/Amey
Ludie   [Possibly a nickname.]
Litha or Lutha
Laura/Laurah/Lora/Laurie
Cerena/Serena/Serene/Sarene/Sarena/Sarina
Selah/Sellah/Sela
Rhoda (Roda)—Rhody
Lucinda/Loucinda or Lucinday—Lou/Loo/Lue/Lu or Cinda
Louvenia or Luevina—Lou or Lu/Lue
Louise—Lou or Lu/Lue
Louisa or Louisi/Luisa/Lueza—Lou or Lu/Lue
Lucretia/Lacresha—Lou or Lu/Lue
Frances—Frankie
Cora/Corah
Aura

Barah
Livinia/Lavinia/Lavania or Lavonia or Lavina
Meola
Stella
Tilda/Tildah
Dathula
Eulalia/Eulalie—Uke or Lolly   [The nickname of one of the author's aunts was Uke.]
Cesaria
Nerva
Henrietta/Henrieta—Henny or Henrie or Netta
Mahala
Penina/Penine—Nina   [Pronounced Pen-neen-ah and Pen-nine-ah. Nina pronounced nine-ah or neen-ah]
Dathney
Vina/Vinah
Margaret (Marguritt)—Peggy/Peggie or Maggie/Magee or Mag or Meg
Lorenza/Larenza
Saphronia/Zaphronia
Sophronia
Lois
Emaline/Emmaline/Emoline/Emiline—Emma
Keziah/Kezia/Keeziah/Kissiah/Kesiah
Keturah/Ketura/K'turah
Anna/Annah/Ana—Annie or Anney/Aney
Hannah/Hanna—Annie
Rosanna/Rosannah—Rose or Anna or Annie
Colleen/Coleen
Della—Del
Fernandella—Della or /Dell/Del
Adeline/Adline—Dell or Addy/Addie
Adella/Adelia—Dell or Del
Mordella—Dell or Del

Fidella—Dell or Del   [Pronounced feye-DEL-ah]
Ardella/Ardell—Dell or Del
Dorree/Dorah
Dorabell—Dora or Belle
Phedora—Dora
Theodora—Dora
Isodore/Isodora/Isedora/Isidor—Dora
Medora—Dora
Inez/Ines
Inesmere—Ines
Alma
Mopsie [Possibly a nickname]
Frieda/Freeda/Freedia/Freda
Elsa—Elsie/Alsie/Alsey/Elsy/Ilsy/Ailsy (Ailsey)
Lavernia   [Also LaVernia]
Beatrice/Beatriss/Beattress/Beattriss—Bea
Aba
Caledonia—Callie
Sabra
Bertha/Birtha—Birthie
Arcada
Eugenia/Uginia—Eugenie/Ugine   [Origin of nickname Jenny?]
Leticia/Lutetia/Letitia/Laticia/Lutecia/Latitia/Luticia—Letty or Leta
Lula/Lulah
Irma
Anastasia/Anastacia
Isabella/Izabella—Belle
Isabel/Ysabel—Belle
Arabella—Belle
Madelline   [Pronounced both mad-uh-lin or mad-uh-line]
Harriet/Heriet
Jemima/Jemimah
Josephine/Josaphine—Jodie or Joe or Josie/Josey

Josepha/Josephe/Josefa
Mabel/Mable
Linelle—Nell or Nel
Thoersa
Phillipa
Matilda/Mathilda—Mattie
Martha—Mattie/Mat
Narcissa/Narcisa/Narsissa/Norcissa or Narcissis/Norcissi—Narcissary/Nurcissey
Amelia   [Pronounced both ah-MEEL-ee-ah or am-MEL-ee-ah]
Elvina
Lulu
Clarissa/Clerissa
Elizabeth/ElisabethEllisabeth—Eliza/Ilisa/Iliza or Liza or Betsy or Bess/Bessie or Libby or Beth or Betty/Bettie or Bet or Liz/Lizzie/Lizzy [But not the modern Lisa]
Amoretta
Gertrude/Gurtrude—Gertie/Gert
Nadeen
Amanda–Mandy/Mande or Manda
Armanda/Armandah
Lea/Leah   [Pronounced Lee-ah]
Paralee/Parolee/Pareley/Parilee or Parlee—Lee
Emma—Em
Viola/Violah or Biola   [Pronounced V-eye-oh-lah]—Vi
Tabitha—Tabby   [Times have changed. Now "Tabby" is for cats!]
Abigail—Abbie/Abby   [Did not encounter the nickname "Gail" in 1870-1900]
Huldah/Hulda/Halda—Huldy
Julie—Jules
Faye/Fay   [Often used in combination with other names as in Wilda Fay]
Ethel
Etheldred—Ethel
Clementine/Clementina/Clemanthia

Drucilla/Drucille (Drucila)—Dru   [Pronounced Drew]
Cilla
Naomi
Angela—Angie
Gladys/Gladis
Rhea
Myrtle or Mirtle
Clara/Clarah
Claire/Clare
Vinnie
Zelma/Zalma
Myra/Mirah
Melvina
Eula
Edith/Eddith
Flora—Flo/Floe or Flossie
Floradora—Flo or Flossie or Dora
Florence/Florance/Florenz or Forence—Flo or Flossie
Zerelda/Zeralda/Zerilda (or Zerrelda)
Blanche/Blanch
Sally/Salli—variant Sally Ann
Zilpha—Zilfie/Zilphie
Minna
Manerly
Arminta—Minnie
Araminta/Arominta—Arrie or Mintie
Marietta
Agnes/Agnis
Adelaide—Addy
Maybelline
Jabez
Ella/Ela/Ellie
Estalene—Stella

Lola
Helen/Helena/Hellen/Helene
Maude/Maud
Ida
Camile
Velma
Clementine
Belinda
Tyra
Hephsibeth
Jerusha
Abidah
Net   [a slave name]
Hester
Twila
Zula/Zala
Sybll
Lydia/Lyddia   (Liddia)
Nina   [Pronounced NINE-ah or NEE-nah]
Zilphia
Letha or Leithy
Sophie/Sophia
Sephronia/Safronia or Safroney/Safrony
Priscilla/Percila/Percilla—Priss
Wilda
Nannita
Charlotte/Charlot/Sharlott/Sharlot/Sharlet/Sharlotte or Charlottee—Charl
Emilia—Emily
Comelia—Emily
Nancy/Nancie—Nannie or Nan
Philomina/Philomena—Lee
Artha
Sevena

Phyllis/Phillis/Philles (Fillis)
Taletha
Lena/Lenna
Madena—Maddie
Carinda
Delores/Deloris
Almira/Elmira/Elmirah
Etheldred—Ethel
Lotta/Lotte
Leslie
Livy/Livey
Cynthia/Sinthia/Cinthia—Sinthy
Scintha
Dolly   [Also widely used as a nickname, especially for "Caroline," it seems]
Artimis—Artemissa/Artimisa/Arthemisia/Årthemesa/Artemisa/Artemissia
Kinzy/Kinsy/Kinsey   [Also a nickname?]
Carla
Wilhelmina/Wilhamina or Whilhelmina (Whilhelminia)
Tallulah/Tollulah/Tolula/Talula
Verona
Vivian/Vivien
Lorissa/Larissa/Loressa/Larisa
Enema   [No kidding! A probable spelling error, different pronunciation, or it may not have had the same meaning then.]
Dorcas/Darkus/Darcus/Darcos/Dorkus
Celia/Selia
Lorinda/Lurinda—Lorrie
Nola
Pilar/Pillar   [Pronounced PEE-lar. A pretty name, in the author's opinion.]
Jeanette/Jenett/Jinnett (Jenette)

Feliciana—Anna or Felice
Winifred—Winnie
Hibbette
Tabusha
Brigit/Bridgid/Brigid/Brigette/Bridgette—Birdy/Birdie/Birdye or Bird or Bridey
Beverley/Beverly
Lucretia—Lucy
Lucilla/Loucilla—Lucy or Cilla
Wherta
Nara
Eulah
Jocaline
Corilla—Rilla
Edison
Mollie/Molly   [Also often used as a nickname.]
Effie/Effy/Effa
Candace/Candis (Candise)—Candy
Vera/Verah
Carrie/Carry//Cary
Ada/Adah/Adda
Theodosia/Theadoshia
Lavender/Lavinder
Patsy/Patsie/Patsey   [Also used as a nickname.]
Cilia
Lensy/Lenzy
Lucia
Scilla
Mintie   [Also used as a nickname for Araminta.]
Mordica
Marinda/Maranda/Marandah/Marindah/Miranda
Melinda/Malinda
Manda
Madora/Medorah/Midora

Delilah/Delila/Delilia—Lily
Jessie/Jessee
Lisa/Lisah
Cordelia—Del
Celia/Cellie
Pruella
Feriba or Feribie/Fereby/Feraby
Lorena/Lorana/Loreena/Lurana/Lorena/Lorina/Lurina
Lorene   [Pronounced either Lore-EEN-ah or Lore-EEN]
Antoinette/Antonette
Sudie or Suda   [Also a nickname]
Eloisa/Heloise
Macedonia or Macedoni/Macedonie
Albertine
Ellen/Ellin
Cintha
Modena
Juliette/Juliett
Easter
Lethe
Millia
Orenya
Althea
Leodica
Elvira/Elvirah
Sarah Lee/Serilee
Lenora—Nora
Jenora
Neanora
Leonora/Lenora/Lanora—Nora/Norah
Elnora—Nora/Norah
Nora/Norah
Linora—Nora/Norah

Luella/Luela/Lualla—Lue
Ara
Sevela
Margarita/Margeretta
Hoxie
Orlena
Dimetreas/Dimetrias/Dimetress
Vincy
Ophelia/Ofelia
Paulina or Pauline
Atelia
Ione
Bathsheba—Sheba
Bashaba—ShabaBarsheba/Sheba
Aline or Alina
Zora
Roxanna/Roxanne
Rowenna/Roenna or Rowenne
Kisseree/Kisere
Samantha/Semantha/Sementhe/Symanthe/Symantha—Semanthy [But apparently not shortened to "Sam" for a woman in this era]
Tandy
Uzza
Jeptha/Jepatha
Pernella/Pernellia/Pernellie
Nellie/Nelly/Nel/Nell
Nelly Bly [4-yr-old female in Hays, 1880 census ... does that mean Nelly Bly was famous in 1876? Incredible, since the woman remembered as Nelly Bly, Elizabeth Jane Cochran, would have only been 12 years old in 1876.]
Vinette/Vinetta
Arabell

Zilphy
Ambrosia [Another pretty name.]
Sarilda
Pathra
Clarinda/Clarindah
Ina/Inah
Idelia
Lesba
Rosetta
Justa
Novella
Fanny/Fany [A name as well as a nickname]
Dunsie
Olivia/Olivea—Olive or Olly
Ampy
Esther/Ester
Pamela or Pamelia—Pam or Mela or Melia
Cheba/Cheaba [Variant of Sheba]
Sylla
Eleanor/Elinor—Ellie
Kissy
Biddy/Biddie/Bitty [A name not a nickname. Of course, the author did run across "Little Bitty," but that was most likely a nickname. "Little Bit," by the way, was a common nickname for little boys in the West even into the 1960s.]
Lutelia [Prounced both Lah-teel-ee-ah or lah-tell-ee-ah]
Ramona/Romona—Mona
Alva/Alvah
Hetty/Hettie/Hette [Although not an "Old West" example, Hetty Green is the most famous example of this first name.]
Lenita
Asca

Bethany or Bethana/Bethanna/Bethannah—Beth or Anna
Melissa/Malissa/Malisse/MellissaMalissah/Melisah
Desdemona or Desdemore
Francine or Francina
Georgeanne/Georgeann—Georgieann or Georgieanna
Andrea or Andra
Florentine/Florentina—Flor
Cecilia/Secilia/Cecelia
Dorothea/Dorathea [Dorotea]
Lahoma/Laoma
Dorinda
Emzy/Emasee
Essie [A nickname?]
Euphronia
Euphonia
Evaline/Evalina— Eva [Pronounced eh-veh-lin or EVE-uh-lin or EVE-uh-line]
Mila
Teresa/Terresa/Terressa
Arletta
Victoria/Victora
Please
Hennetta
Arthesa
Justina
Rosalie
Sila
Sena
Alpha
Neve
Pursy
Docia/Dosiah
Sedora
Tooka

Lurenza
Tamsey
Mitty   [A name and a nickname]
Orna
Hallie
Bethie   [A name and a nickname]
Lauda
Lindy   [A name and a nickname]
Norma
Dones   [Pronounced dohn-EZ]
Zima
Judith/Judithe
Aquilla
Miniah   [Pronounced man-EYE-ah]
Aranda/Arinda
China
Baby—Babe
Holly
Lilea
Martilena
Tekla
Lolie
Eunice/Unice
Nyla
Talitha
Tula/Tulah—Tulia
Ulna   [Derived from the name of an *arm bone*? The author doesn't think so.]
Zania
Cortney
Casina
Almidy
Rosella—Ella

Liddy
Loraine/Lorraine'Larane/Luraine
Standhope
Evelyn/Eveline
Crochet
Knitter   [Probably a nickname]
Parthone
Sheila/Sheilah (Sheelah)
Roxie
Tina
Mimms—Mimsie/Mimzy or Mim
Marsha
Lean   [Probably a variant spelling of Leeann. Hard to imagine it as Leen]
Ava/Avah
Genet   [But not Janet in this time period]
Mena
Tennersa
Althena
Sinah/Cinah/Cyna
Kezia/Kaziah
Julina
Visa
Vandy
Hyne   [Prounounced HY-nee, believe it or not...!]
Presha
Kate/Cate
Stena
Tilitha
Lura/Lurah
Chipita
Lurity or Lurithy
Ozilla
Gale

Santoree or Santorey
Santore
Denneth
Satina
Anatha
Ima
Zilta
Idel
Griffa
Jennine
Priciliann/Pricillianne
Dee   [A name and a nickname]
Portia
Mamie   [A name and a nickname]
Denia
Finette
Adena
Amsi
Merida/Meridah
Alonette or Alonetta/Alonettah
Lusena
Surrepta
Rosalind/Rosalynd or Rosalynda/Rosalinda—Roz
Rosilin/Rosilyn—Roz
Pennicia—Penny
Sibby
Euphemia/Euphimia—Euphemy
Pernesie
Sythe/Sytha   [Pronounced SI-thah, not sih-tha from the tool]
Renta
Jeba   [Pronounced Jee-bah]
Parthene   [Pronounced Per-theen-ee or par-then-ee]
Delphi   [Pronounced both DEL-fey or DEL-fee]

Tepania
Gregoria
Celestin
Billie/Bili   [One of the mysteries of the author's life is that his *father* was named Billie, not William or Bill or Billy....]
Sernthneta—Netta
Tess or Tessia/Tesiah
Bernia
Euna
Minta
Cridia
Peomelia
Prus
Puss/Pussie   [No kidding, I've encountered this name or nickname a number of times during research ...!]
Alzira
Gwynn
Palmyra
Pertina—Tina
Selma
Didoma
Alpedonia
Lursia
Alphra
Bevela
Delinda
Dushee
Fatima
Lexis—Lexie   [not the name of the car, either]
Marah
Elbet
Josiso
Shemar

Tova
Milta
Lucidy
Laredy
Gally
Burta
Kasiah
Netta
Burta
Kasiah
Netta
Delia
Lace/Lacey
Matha
Andoline
Lemina
Barbara/Barbra
Artitia
Jain
Blythe
Dilzie or Dilsy/Dilsie
Florinda
Orna
Linley
Magdalena/Magtalena—Magda/Magdah
Mizilla
Ulda
Sharon/Zaron
Zaccarinda
Exia
Vinina
Arsene/Arsena/Arsennah
Belzora

Harlit/Harlitt [Hard to imagine someone named this, but there it is....]
Lavinsey/Lavinsay/Lavinsa
Oba
Juda/Judah/Juddah
Lil   [Probably a nickname]
Sherly   [Modern spelling is Shirley after 1900]
Tish
Womba
Zylphia
Lona
Petra
Hortense/Hortens
Johanna
Cleotilde
Aphne
Dellar
Melly
Naoma
Aloizie
Analynn
Leora
Rosella
Philacena
Mozelle/Mozella
Ernstine/Ernestine
Arzelia
Florendine
Jora
Iva
Gussie
Chloe
Minde/Mindy
Neppi

Carietta
Lavonia
Judithella
Albinnie
Almer
Avica
Siorey
Pellie
Mirl/Meryl
Glenys/Glinnis
Elnir
Lowitha
Floy
Malli
Jozaba/Jozabah
Ottilie
Arsuinda
Della
Mertie
Leta/Letha
Celista
Caledonia
Monnie
Amzie
Fern
Froma
Morah
Filora
Dorma
Shrilda
Sarina
Petronilla
Philomena

Melia
Hesta
Celesta
Aryanna
Luevina
Vona
Damaris
Otho
Nancyu
Elsie
Cecelia
Sully   [Both a man's name and a woman's]
Nolie
Veonie
Aletta
Aurena
Lurline
Loleat
Creacy
Arealie
Lura
Desdemona
Larenza
Zeda
Retha
Ouida
Verty
Morelda
Violonia
Talitha
Coloma
Alsabella—Bella or Belle
Sindy

Babette
Paulena
Colma
Albertia
Bithy
Alnonia
Dode/Dodie   [Pronounced doh-dee]
Roszille
Rachil   [Variant of Rachel]
Orly
Deltha
Gadis
Endora
Ruanna/Runannah
Cevillia
Dulcenia/Dulcinia
Bramwell
Alif
Lori
Vorrulia
Ula
Zilla
Theophilia
Cari
Aurry
Odilia
Herloise
Phetna
Mariah
Rubana
Idalee
Helton
Vidalia

Rosabell
Celey
Bethenia-Beth
Pricilla
Morteen
Thomsa
Eletha
Dicey/Dicy
Muria/Moriah
Mosiria
Lavisa
Barba
Amma
Clora
Bragena
Victora
Marria
Tempe/Tempey
Pandora
Pink Cloud
Azalee
Berthena
Sistara
Marilla
Luceta
Latia
Kansas Jane
Plez
Percilla
Evia
Berthena
Allise/
Marium (Mirium)

Telitha
Malisse/Mellissa
Mosira
Vashti
Satira
Ursula/Ursala
Leralda
Classa
Lorensa
Verty
Asula
Adelaida Levalia
Joaline
Seila
Martine
Nula
Asena
Adelaida
Alvina
Terressa
Demaris/Demoris
Sherrida
Mabe
Charrisa
Ludellia
Hiberna
Qua
Delida
Looie
Perima--Ima
Patrina
Laba
Amia

Bitha
Lidinia
Winna
Ferrybie
Telithia
Triphenia/Trifenia
Zonzetta
Haddie
Porthenia
Cardelia
Bastra
Ermiline
Viauna
Phronia
Lallie
Missie/Myssie
Alonsa
Osilla
Altheria
Rue Emma
Lizzea
Lucinderella

WOMEN'S NICKNAMES
Author's Favorite: Featherlegs

Abbie
Lola
Minnie
Bess or Bessie
Eva
Old Mother

Ma
Fat Mama
Mother
Nanny
Baby/Babe
Aunt/Auntie
Grandma
Oomah
Lottie
Camilla or Camille
Flossie
Zee
Hazel
Kitty
Libbie
Tessie or Tess
Lil or Lillie or Lilly
Carrie
Lottie
Lucy
Mattie
Fannie
Mollie
Molly
Aggie
Featherlegs
Nell
Nellie
Dodie
Patsy
Pollie
Polly
Annie

Sadie
Tootsie
Dolly
Stella
Tillie
Toodles
Gussy
Hebe
Dixie
Hettie
Kate
Lulu
Millie
Mixie
Cleo
Bitty
Girlie/Girly
Sheba
Nell/Nel or Nelly/Nellie
Queenie

FAMOUS WOMEN'S NICKNAMES OF THE OLD WEST
Author's Favorite: "Little Egypt"

"Calamity Jane" .... Martha Cannary [Two notes: Jane may not have been Martha Cannary's middle name, and, secondly, the nickname "Calamity Jane" was used by several women of the Old West.]

"Baby Doe" Tabor [May have started out as a prostitute]

"Old Mother Featherlegs" Shephard

"Big Nose Kate" .... Mary Katherine Horony Elder

"Molly B'Damn"	Maggie Burdan
"Madame Mustache"	Eleanora Dumont
"Poker Alice"	Alice Ivers Duffield Tubbs Huckert
"Sweet Pea Girl"	Rose Tiffany Bechtol
"Little Egypt"	Fahruda Manzar
"Unsinkable" Molly Brown	Margaret "Molly" Brown
"Little Sure-Shot	Annie Oakley
"Rose of the Cimarron"	Rose Elizabeth [Ella?] Dunn Fleming
"The Messenger of Defeat"	Susan A. Dickinson [Dickerson] Hannig, woman survivor of the battle of the Alamo in 1836]
"The Babe of the Alamo"	Angelina Dickinson
"Cattle Annie"	Emmaline Anna Roach, outlaw
"Little Britches"	Jennie Stevens or Jennie Stenenson, outlaw
"Cattle Kate"	Kate Maxwell and Ellen Liddy Watson
"Ella" Watson	Ellen Liddy Watson, lynched in Wyoming, 1889
Annie Skeggs	A Virginia City, Montana madam
Slue-Foot Sue	Fictional character Pecos Bill's wife
"Nelly Bly" or "Pinky"	Elizabeth Cochrane Seaman
"Ma" Ferguson	Governor Miriam Ferguson
"Cattle Kate"	Ellen Liddy Watson
"Ma'am" Jones	Barbara Jones [After her death, "Ma'am Jones of the Pecos"]
"Cattle Kate"	Ella Watson
"Little Sure Shot," "Annie Oakley"	Phoebe Ann Moses/Mosey
"Princess Wenona"	Lillian Frances Smith
"Little Egypt"	[Three women, Fahreda Mazar Spyropoulos, Catherine Devine (aka Ashea Wabe), and Fatima Djemille, danced under this name]
"Hurricane Minnie"	Minnie Martin
"Baby Doe"	Elizabeth Bonduel (McCourt) Tabor

"Calamity Jane"   Martha Jane Canary
"Angel of the Battlefield"   Clara Barton
May "The Silhouette Girl" Leslie
Sophia Treadway Reavis—"Doñ a Maria Micaela Maso Reavis y Peralta de la Cordoba"

NAMES AND NICKNAMES OF WOMEN OF "EASY VIRTUE"

Author's Favorite: "The Sweet Pea Girl" [Though Sweet Pea Girl was a well known prostitute, the author's favorite was THE Sweet Pea Girl, not a prostitute, but a woman we might call a "groupie" today: Rosalind Bowers

FAMOUS NAMES OR NICKNAMES:

Mag Wood	[A Caldwell, Kansas, madam]
Mattie Silks	
Martha A. Ready	[A Denver, Colorado, madam]
Lottie Deno	Carlotta J. Thompkins, gambler
Lola Montez	Marie Dolores Eliza Rosanna Gilbert
Jo DeMerritt	
Veronica Baldwin	
Lil Lovell	[A Denver, Colorado, madam]
Etta Clark	[An El Paso, Texas, madam]
Tillie Howard	[An El Paso, Texas, madam]
"Calamity Jane"	Martha Cannary [Jane may not have been her middle name]
"Kentucky Daisy"	Nannita Daisy
"Baby Doe" Tabor	[May have started out as a prostitute]
"Rowdy Kate"	[A Wichita madam]
Jennie Rogers	Leeah J. Wood, a Denver, Colorado madam

"Big Nose Kate" .... Mary Katherine Horony Elder
"Molly B'Damn" .... Maggie Burdan
"Dirty Em"
"Madame Mustache" .... Eleanora Dumont
"Madame Bull Dog" .... Kitty O'Leary
"Poker Alice" .... Tubbs [Ivers]
"Diamond Lil" .... Davenport
"Diamond Tooth Lil" .... Honora Ornstein
"Sweet Pea Girl" .... Rose Tiffany Bechtol
"Gypsy Queen" .... Monroe
"The Turkish Whirlwind Daneuse" Freda Malof
"Gussie" .... Grace Anderson
"Dirty Maud" .... Delisle
"Little Egypt" .... see below
"The Hootchy-Kootchy Girl" Farida Mazar Spyropoulos [Also called "Little Egypt," not known to have been in the West ... but famous all over the West!]

Moll Featherlegs [A Virginia City, Montana madam]
Annie Skegs [A Virginia City, Montana madam]
"Cock-Eyed Liz" [A Buena Vista, Colorado madam, possibly born as Lizzie Spurgen]

Pearl DeVere [A Cripple Creek, Colorado madam]
"Diamond Bessie" Annie Stone/Bessie Moore

NAMES OF THE NOT-SO-FAMOUS:

Chesty/Chestie
Snook 'Ems/Snookums/Snooks
Sugar
Giddy Girl
Little Annie

Big Annie
Big Em
Big Hattie
Big Mouth
Diamond Girl
Black Hills Annie, Rachel or Betty, etc.
Buffalo Hump   [An Indian name. Not sure about the "modern" context...]
Worthless
Worthless Girl
Belle
Belle Fourche
Lady   [Also Lady Gay, not the modern sense/Lady Ann, etc.]
Sweet Pea   [Also Sweet Annie, Lou, Ruby, etc.]
Angel
Angel Girl
Lucky/Luckie
Beautiful Baby/Girl
Goldie/Goldy
Girlie/Girly
Queen/Queenie
Contrary Girl
Sheba/Shebah
Baby/Babe/Babie
Vinnie   [From Vinnola?]
Dugie
Dugs
Pretty Polly   [Also Annie, Alice, Willa, etc.]
Sad Girl   [Sounds counter-productive for attracting customers...]
Sadie
China Girl
Billie

Tish
Raspberry Girl
U.S. Dollar
Chicago Lil or Betty
Cock-Eye[d] Liz or Annie, etc.
One-Eye[d] Annie etc.
Panhandle
Klondike Girl
Cum Chow   [A prostitute in San Francisco in 1880; another prostitute was Kum Chow]
Ho Chow   [A prostitute in San Francisco in 1880]
You Fok   [A prostitute in Kern, California in 1880]
Lee Fuck   [A prostitute in San Francisco in 1880]
Lady Ann
Lady Luck
Doll
Beautiful Doll
Dutch Annie, etc.
English Gussie, etc.
French Kate or Annie, etc.
German Girl or Kate, etc.
Irish Ann or Kate, etc.
Jew Ann or Jessie, etc.
Mexican Maria, etc.
Santa Fe Girl
Santa Fe Trale   [Spelling encountered twice]
Spanish Girl or Maria, etc.
Big Cow
Peg-Leg
Rowdy Ann or Kate, etc.
Little Girl   [A pederast's target? Or a name?]
Little Annie or Betty, etc.
Dollar Girl

The Pig   [Variation "The pig" Annie or "The pig" Kate, etc.]
Peek-a-boo Girl [or Peek-a-boo]
Sweet Ann or Sweet Kate, etc.
Bad Girl
Fat/Fatty Girl or Fat/Fatty Annie
Lucinderella
Leontine
Eggie
Franke   [Pronounced Frank-ee]
Louease   [Pronounced Louise}
Filicite/Feliciti
Dena
Alfa
Dada
Sug—Suggie
Peninah   [Prononunced two ways: Pen-IN-a or pen-een-ah]

BLACK WOMEN'S GIVEN NAMES

Siby
Wennie
Vira
Ladora
Illinois (Especially seen among blacks in 1870s and '80s. Was this a symbolic name?)
Mety
Feranna (black female)
Haga
Cooney
Freedom (Touching name of a 14-yr-old black female, Freedom Bell, 1880 Texas census, Gonzales Co., born just after Emancipation)
Meloini

Lusilia
Jenishe
Precilla
Nicey
Grocie
Zue   [Prounced both Sue and Zoo-ey]
Toodles
Aurinda
Kettey
Kizzie
Rubelia
Gilespia
Cinderela
Bunnera
Sibbie
Chanc
Relda

HISPANIC WOMEN'S GIVEN NAMES
Author's Favorite: Esperanza (Though Dulce is a sweet name!)

Note: Again, I am confronted with the disparate routes to the U.S. The eastern route (border and central Mexico to Texas) is dominated by Eurpoean names: Carmen, Maria, Olivia, Yeraldin, Luisa) and the west route (western Mexico and Sonora to California) by these names:

Carmina
Ancelara
Genara
Efigenia
Trinidad
Tomasa/Tomesa

Refugia
Luisa
Urbana
Hilaria
Pilar
Romula
Urbana
Dulce
Eusebia
Prudencia
Candelaria
Hilaria
Lacera
Milchra/Milchera
Soledad
Secumbria
Sena
Gusfa
Ysabel/Isabel
Ventura
Torriba
Romulda
Tasimera
Selima
Romez
Appolinaria
Ventura
Dolima
Chonah
Kitiana
Nicolasa
Nelphine
Honorine

Adolphine
Loupe
Pioquinta
Fanchos
Casimira
Chriselda
Anofra
Azinte
Maryquita
Cayetana
Diocelina
Ninfa

MISCELLANEOUS WOMEN'S NAMES:

April
May/Mae
June
Cherry
Daisy/Daisie/Daise/Dasie/Dasie
Ivory   [Of the examples I've encountered during research, the majority of the women named Ivory were black women.]
Sister—Sissie or Sis   [A name, but also a nickname or title]
Polka
Temple
Ginger
Ivy/Ive
Dove
Monday
Tuesday
Friday
Easter

SURNAMES

Author's Favorite: Champion
Most Ethnic: Lzezinklenskie [From 1880 Texas Census]

Today's familiar surnames were, for the most part, names of the Old West too. For example, Jackson, Davis, McLeod, Shaeffer, Grimes, Farris, Walters, Morris, Nash, James, Hempstead, Goins, Tabor, Cox ... and McCown ... were all names commonly encountered in research on the Old West.

Another facet of surnames must be acknowledged. The mid to late-19th century was a time of tremendous immigration to the United States. Large ethnic groups moved into the West and maintained their identities throughout this time period. The result, for screenwriters and other writers, is that ethnic names are quite common. In Texas, for example, colonies of Irish, Germans, Wends, Poles, Czechs, and Norwegians dominated large sections of the state. In Colorado, Italian and Welsh names predominated in the mining districts. In California, Chinese names were common to the time period, and in Wyoming, English cattle barons and Irish railroad workers were common. So, names that the author has never seen in today's world like Griffenstein, Lingenfelter,

Slumzchorisag, Bickenbach, Luxsinger/Lucksinger, Klenzendorff, Quattlebaum, Radenslebery, and others have either died out or been Anglicized over the last hundred years.

Therefore, this short list contains period names that the author finds interesting because:

1.) The author DOESN'T encounter these names in today's world.
2.) The names are common in the Old West
3.) The names are just plain fascinating

Beebe	Glossbrenner	Osteen
Tays/Teas	DeGraffenreid	Parminter
Pardee	Nebo	Modgling
Mogoffin	Mimms	Renfro
Favorite	Lanihan	Paralee
Pascoe	Sallee	Ringgold/Ringo
Slorah	Withers	Rudabaugh
Champion	Chisholm/Chisum	Rickabaugh
Illingworth/Illingsworth	Durfee	Whetstone
Bledsoe	Shilgo	DuFran
Lincecum	Sunday	Fristoe
Duderstadt	Martindale	Shegog
Goodbread	Mayhill/Myhill	Labushe
Hollybee	McGinty	Dragg
McQuigg	Koonson	Bomar
Schoonover	Blaylock	Goldenbagen
Loveless	Fullilove	Lovelady
Livengood	Livesay	LeDoux
Heppinstall/Heppistall	Shadoin	Rideout
Fennessey	Misenheimer	Laughter
Lott	Horrell	Murff
Zimpelman/Zimpelmann	Lisendecker/Lysendecker	LaHeridge

Hatchett	Landermilk	Wisterfeldt
Finney	Plowman	Neatherlin

And Tennille [Pronounced ten-ill. Modern Old West aficionados misprounce it as ten eel, probably because of the singing duo, Captain and Tennille]

DESCRIPTIVE NAMES

ALTERNATIVE NAMES FOR WHISKEY—

Old Pump and Pull
Old Rabbit's Foot
Pull-and-Rye   [Probably Pull-<u>on</u>-Rye in real conversation]
Gag It Down
Forty Rod Bug Juice
Old Tanglefoot
Dance and Fall [also Dance-and-Drop or Dance-'n-Trip]
Tin-Top
Long Horn/Longhorn
Frosty [and Old Frosty]
I-see, I-didn't, I-can't
White Mule
Mule Spark
Mule Kick
Pain 'n Hurt
The Mule
Sparkle
Dazzle/Dazzle King/Razzle Dazzle

Punch [perhaps a concotion]
Drop
Kick 'Em

ALTERNATIVE NAMES FOR BARS—

The Road To Ruin
Holy Moses [also Holy Mose]
Silver King
Golden Saddle/Gold Saddle
Jersey Lilly [also misspelled as Jersy Lily etc.]
First Chance
Last Chance

Best Chance
Dirty Dog
Mule Skinner
Bull's Head   [A famous saloon not referencing part of a bull with horns]
Bucket of Blood   [aka The Bucket of Blood]
Arcade/The Arcade
Birdcage
The Buckhorn [The Antler/ Forked Antler/Antler]
Lone Tree/Single Tree
Spicy Lady
Long Branch/Dry Branch/Lost Branch
Summer
Winter's Retreat
Northern/Southern
Northern Branch/Southern Branch
Red Dog [Dawg]/Red Horse/Red Indian/ Red's
Red Man
Teepee/Tipi

Wild Horse
Longhorn
Cattle King [also Cattle plus names like Cattle Dick or Kate etc.]
Cowboy/Cow-boy
Alpine
Echo
Crystal Palace
White Elephant [Elephant]
Empire [The Imperial or Royal/Regal]
Discovery/Discover
Blue Ribbon/ Red Ribbon
Pioneer
Bank Saloon
Salty Dog [Dawg]
Red Onion
Estancia
El Rancho
Sourdough
Klondike [Klondyke]
Golden Crown/Gold Crown
Golden Nugget/The Gold Nugget
Crown/Triple Crown
Shamrock
Irish Curse   [Irish Luck encountered just once, but included here]
Scot's Glee
Happy Jack's
Crazy Jack's
Crazy Loon
Kick-in-the-Pants
Shiloh
The Boot
Grand Palace [Palace and The Palace]
The Irma
Dodge [The Dodge]

Stella's
Sally's
Patsy Anne's
Pawnee
Shoshoni
The Arapaho
Lookout
Bisbee
No-Account
Sheridan
Border Town
Laredo
Tucson
El Paso
Paso del Norte
Nogales
Yuma
Washoe [Old Washoe]
Dimebox [Old Dimebox, New Dimebox]
Llano
Cheyenne
Damned Shame [Darn Shame seems to be exclusively modern]
Lone Star
Dexter [also Dexter House]
Rancho
Lariat/Lasso
Saddleblanket
Cowboy's Haven [also Cowboy's Rest]
San Juan
Acme
Zenith
Pinnacle
Peak

Mountaintop   [also Mountain Top]
1900
Gold Pan
Blue Front
Phenix
Laramie
Old Town/New Town
Cactus/Yucca/Lone Tree/Big Tree/Pine Tree
Diamond
Buckshot
Shotgun
Paradise
Heaven
Hell on Wheels
Hell's Retreat
I am Coming
The Outlaw[s]
The Exchange [Buckhorn Exchange]
Capitol/Capital [The Capitol]
Elixir
Barbary Coast
Spur   [Silver Spur/Texas Spur/Mexican Spur, etc.]
Wet Your Whistle [Wet Yer Whistle]
Liquid   [Liquid Emporium]
Graveyard   [no kidding!]
Regular
Home [Our Home/Your Home/Home's Rest]
Dry   [Dry No More encountered once, referring to a hovel near Ft. Laramie, but pretty cool, so I break my "5 times" rule]
Hog Ranch
Whore Hole Saloon
Branch/Dry Branch/North Branch/South Branch

North Fork/South Fork/Middle Fork/Dry Fork/Seco
Lost
Buck the Tiger
Lion
Stampede
The Revenge
Horseshoe/Golden Horseshoe/Silver Horseshoe/Muleshoe
Falls/The Falls
Townhall/Courthouse/Court House
Law 'n Order
Cain't Shock
Western
Bowler
Coney Island
World's Fair [Chicago World's Fair encountered only once in Manhattan, Kansas]
Six Gun
Pistolero/Pistol
Junction [many variations of this, such as Llano Junction]
Pike's Peak
Yellowstone   [many variations of this, such as Yellowstone Peak]
Big Horn
Ruby   [Ruby's]
Pearl   [The Pearl]
Liberal/The Liberal
Upstairs/Downstairs
Next Door
Neighbor [The Neighbor]
Hard Mine/Deep Mine
Family/My Family
The No Name [No Name/No-Name]
Champion
Top Dog

SLIPPERY JACK

Wigwam
The #1
The Number Two
Sleepy
Dream/Dreamy
Star/North Star
Orion
Marshal['s]
Skull
Bones/Leg Bone
Host Club

UNUSUAL NAMES

NAMES FROM RESEARCH—

We finished the 2010 Census a few years ago. By chance, I was running an Adult Education class in a public library in Austin, Texas. Literally outside my door in the library sat a census worker prepared to answer questions—and I overheard some pretty bizarre ones, let me tell you! Were our ancestors in the Old West as reluctant to deal with a once-in-a-decade civic duty? Were they as suspicious about the government collecting personal information? Or did they deal with the census in humor? I think they were no different than us. Some interesting names and nicknames popped up during my research that are memorable. This happened over and over during my research in Texas for another book. In a state legendary for Governor James Stephen Hogg naming his daughter Ima comes a few examples, these from the 1880 census:

Camel Monday
Sinah Pooper
Ruff & Ready Piler
Read Page
Bile Pain
Orange Payne

Pink Payne
Blooming Parkhill
Dr. Green Peay
Honey Peel
Glassville Sharp
Funney Price
Wash Raines
Odd Riddle
Isabud Rose
Rose Rose
Silly Sanders
Black Smith
Drue Sila [similar to first name Drucilla]
Hap Sing [Having grown up on the television series *Bonanza*, I was surprised to find the name actually existed in the Old West!]
Sam Sam
Coon Roundtree   [A black man. May have been a nickname. Racist? Probably not, if he had himself ennumerated with the name ….]
Caspian Seay
Easy Self
Noble King
Nero Nero
William William
Pink Green

Plus:

Almon D. Fudge—Texas Civil War Muster Rolls

www.ingramcontent.com/pod-product-compliance
Lightning Source LLC
Chambersburg PA
CBHW071719090426
42738CB00009B/1818